3.600 PALABRAS CLAVE DEL INGLÉS

DEL INGLÉS

Expresiones y conceptos básicos

Autor: Richard Vaughan

Coordinación del proyecto: Rubén Palomero

© Vaughan Systems S.L., 2014
C/ Orense 69, 1ª planta
28020 Madrid
Tel.: 91 444 58 44
Fax: 91 444 58 36
www.vaughantienda.com

Depósito legal: B-18765-2014
Impreso en España / Printed in Spain
Imprenta: Rotäbook
© Vaughan Systems S.L., Madrid – 2014.

Consigue otros títulos de la colección
"Inglés que deberías conocer"

Vocabulary booklet 1
NIVEL PRINCIPIANTE

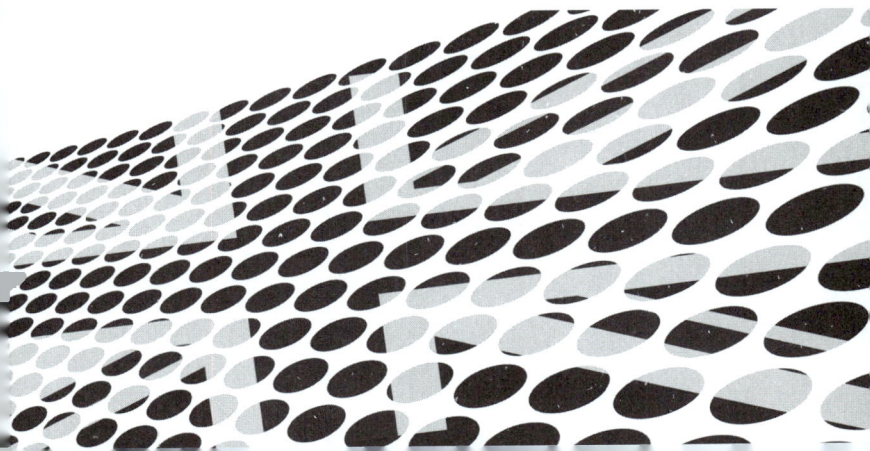

LIST 1

	MANZANA	APPLE
	MALO	BAD
	GRANDE	BIG
	NEGRO	BLACK
	AZUL	BLUE
	LIBRO	BOOK
	MUCHACHO	BOY
	COCHE	CAR
	GATO	CAT
	SILLA	CHAIR
	CIUDAD	CITY
	CLASE	CLASS
	PERRO	DOG
	BIEN	FINE
	MUCHACHA	GIRL
	BUENO	GOOD
	CASA	HOUSE
	NOMBRE	NAME
	BOLIGRAFO	PEN
	LAPIZ	PENCIL
	TELEFONO	PHONE
	PEQUEÑO	SMALL
	ESTACIÓN	STATION
	CALLE	STREET
	APARCAR	TO PARK

	APARTAMENTO, PISO	APARTMENT
	CERVEZA	BEER
	BOTELLA	BOTTLE
	MARRON	BROWN
	CALENDARIO	CALENDAR
	RELOJ (DE MESA O PARED)	CLOCK
	PAIS, CAMPO	COUNTRY
	MESA DE TRABAJO	DESK
	PUERTA	DOOR
	FRANCIA	FRANCE
	FRANCES	FRENCH
	SOMBRERO	HAT
	ITALIA	ITALY
	IDIOMA	LANGUAGE
	LECCION	LESSON
	PERIODICO	NEWSPAPER
	NUMERO	NUMBER
	OFICINA	OFFICE
	PAPEL	PAPER
	CUADRO, FOTO	PICTURE
	ALUMNO	STUDENT
	AZUCAR	SUGAR
	MESA	TABLE
	ESE, ESO, AQUEL, AQUELLO	THAT
	ESTE, ESTO	THIS

LIST 3

	AEROPUERTO	AIRPORT
	CONTESTACIÓN, RESPUESTA	ANSWER
	CAMA	BED
	CAJA	BOX
	CIGARRILLO	CIGARETTE
	CORRECTO	CORRECT
	TAZA	CUP
	DICIEMBRE	DECEMBER
	VESTIDO	DRESS
	FACIL	EASY
	FAMILIA	FAMILY
	ADIOS	GOOD BYE
	VERDE	GREEN
	AQUI	HERE
	CABALLO	HORSE
	MARIDO	HUSBAND
	ITALIANO	ITALIAN
	LARGO	LONG
	HOMBRE, SEÑOR	MAN
	CUADERNO, BLOC	NOTEBOOK
	PLATO	PLATE
	BONITO	PRETTY
	RIO	RIVER
	ESCUELA, COLEGIO	SCHOOL
	BARCO	SHIP

	UNA NECESIDAD	A NEED
	TARDE (DESPUES DE MEDIODIA)	AFTERNOON
	DORMITORIO	BEDROOM
	PAJARO	BIRD
	LIMPIO	CLEAN
	CAFE	COFFEE
	ALEMAN	GERMAN
	BOLSO	HANDBAG
	DEBERES (DE CLASE)	HOMEWORK
	CALUROSO, CALIENTE	HOT
	HORA	HOUR
	DELANTE DE	IN FRONT OF
	REVISTA	MAGAZINE
	MAPA, PLANO	MAP
	ESTRECHO	NARROW
	NUEVO	NEW
	AL LADO DE	NEXT TO
	AGRADABLE	NICE
	SECRETARIA	SECRETARY
	TIENDA	SHOP
	CORTO, BAJO	SHORT
	HERMANA	SISTER
	LENTO	SLOW
	FUERTE	STRONG
	TREN	TRAIN

LIST 5

BRAZO	ARM
BANCO	BANK
JEFE	BOSS
NIÑOS, HIJOS	CHILDREN
AULA	CLASSROOM
ABRIGO	COAT
FLOR	FLOWER
ALEMANIA	GERMANY
IDEA	IDEA
ENERO	JANUARY
LUZ	LIGHT
MINUTO	MINUTE
ERROR	MISTAKE
MONTAÑA	MOUNTAIN
BOCA	MOUTH
PLANTA	PLANT
SILENCIOSO	QUIET
ROJO	RED
HABITACION	ROOM
CANSADO	TIRED
DEBAJO DE	UNDER
MUY	VERY
CAMARERO	WAITER
PARED, MURO	WALL
AGUA	WATER

	ENTRE	AMONG
	ENFADADO	ANGRY
	DESAYUNO	BREAKFAST
	FRIO	COLD
	PADRE	FATHER
	PEZ, PESCADO	FISH
	BOSQUE	FOREST
	FRUTA	FRUIT
	PELO	HAIR
	DURO	HARD
	CABEZA	HEAD
	JULIO	JULY
	LAMPARA	LAMP
	IZQUIERDA	LEFT
	MERCADO	MARKET
	MADRE	MOTHER
	RUIDOSO	NOISY
	PLAN	PLAN
	PREGUNTA, CUESTION	QUESTION
	ENFERMO	SICK
	HIJO	SON
	ALTO	TALL
	PROFESOR	TEACHER
	TELEFONO	TELEPHONE
	RELOJ	WATCH

LIST 7

	OTRO	ANOTHER
	ARTE	ART
	EDIFICIO	BUILDING
	PERO	BUT
	IGLESIA	CHURCH
	OSCURO	DARK
	EJEMPLO	EXAMPLE
	ARCHIVO, EXPEDIENTE	FILE
	SUELO	FLOOR
	VIERNES	FRIDAY
	JAMON	HAM
	HAMBRIENTO	HUNGRY
	LLAVE, CLAVE	KEY
	MAQUINA	MACHINE
	CERCA DE	NEAR
	NECESARIO	NECESSARY
	PERSONA	PERSON
	POBRE	POOR
	PROBLEMA	PROBLEM
	RADIO	RADIO
	LISTO, PREPARADO	READY
	SIMILAR	SIMILAR
	MUJER	WOMAN
	AÑO	YEAR
	JOVEN	YOUNG

	ACERCA DE, SOBRE	ABOUT
	SEÑAS, DIRECCION	ADDRESS
	DESPUES DE	AFTER
	DETRAS DE	BEHIND
	ENTRE	BETWEEN
	BARATO	CHEAP
	DIFICIL	DIFFICULT
	SUCIO	DIRTY
	JUEGO	GAME
	GUANTE	GLOVE
	DIA FESTIVO	HOLIDAY
	IMPORTANTE	IMPORTANT
	EL JAPON	JAPAN
	CLASE, TIPO	KIND
	LIMON	LEMON
	LEON	LION
	SALON, CUARTO DE ESTAR	LIVING ROOM
	NARIZ	NOSE
	PADRES	PARENTS
	CERDO	PIG
	POSIBLE	POSSIBLE
	PROGRAMA	PROGRAM
	RATA	RAT
	DE VERDAD	REALLY
	INFORME	REPORT

LIST 9

	ALREDEDOR DE	AROUND
	PAN	BREAD
	TECHO	CEILING
	ORDENADOR	COMPUTER
	DIA	DAY
	SECO	DRY
	EUROPA	EUROPE
	RAPIDO	FAST
	PASILLO	HALL
	REUNION	MEETING
	DINERO	MONEY
	MES	MONTH
	MUSICA	MUSIC
	NERVIOSO	NERVOUS
	RUIDO	NOISE
	FIESTA	PARTY
	GENTE	PEOPLE
	BOLSILLO	POCKET
	PUERTO (DE MAR)	PORT
	PROGRESO	PROGRESS
	HISTORIA, CUENTO	STORY
	SEMANA	WEEK
	BIEN	WELL
	ANCHO	WIDE
	VENTANA	WINDOW

	HERMOSO	BEAUTIFUL
	AUTOBUS	BUS
	PELIGROSO	DANGEROUS
	FECHA	DATE
	DIBUJO	DRAWING
	GORDO	FAT
	FEBRERO	FEBRUARY
	PRIMERO	FIRST
	VASO, VIDRIO, CRISTAL	GLASS
	EMPLEO, TRABAJO, TAREA	JOB
	TARDE	LATE
	LINEA	LINE
	AFORTUNADO	LUCKY
	PARQUE	PARK
	LLAMADA TELEFONICA	PHONE CALL
	AVION	PLANE
	PROFESIONAL	PROFESSIONAL
	RICO	RICH
	FRASE	SENTENCE
	SISTEMA	SYSTEM
	ARBOL	TREE
	¿ POR QUE ?	WHY ?
	ESPOSA	WIFE
	VINO	WINE
	CON	WITH

LIST 11

MUCHO, MUCHOS	A LOT OF
AREA, ZONA	AREA
PRINCIPIANTE	BEGINNER
RUBIO	BLOND
LIBRERIA	BOOKSHOP
MANTEQUILLA	BUTTER
QUESO	CHEESE
CLARO, TRANSPARENTE	CLEAR
VACA	COW
HIJA	DAUGHTER
DIFERENTE, DISTINTO	DIFFERENT
ABAJO, HACIA ABAJO	DOWN
ESTE	EAST
ELEFANTE	ELEPHANT
OJO	EYE
INCENDIO, FUEGO	FIRE
NIEBLA	FOG
AMIGO	FRIEND
GARAJE	GARAGE
PEQUEÑO	LITTLE
LECHE	MILK
PAGINA	PAGE
PRECIO	PRICE
TEMA	SUBJECT
GRUESO, ESPESO	THICK

	Spanish	English
	ACCIDENTE	ACCIDENT
	TODO, TODOS	ALL
	EN CASA	AT HOME
	HERMANO	BROTHER
	VIAJE DE NEGOCIOS	BUSINESS TRIP
	ROPA	CLOTHES
	ALGODON	COTTON
	COMEDOR	DINING ROOM
	OIDO, OREJA	EAR
	CADA, TODOS	EVERY
	CARA	FACE
	PIE	FOOT
	MANO	HAND
	ALTO	HIGH
	HOTEL	HOTEL
	¿ CUANTOS ?	HOW MANY ?
	¿ CUANTO ?	HOW MUCH ?
	LA INDIA	INDIA
	MUCHOS	MANY
	CARNE	MEAT
	PELICULA	MOVIE
	CAMINO, CARRETERA	ROAD
	NIEVE	SNOW
	SOPA	SOUP
	SORPRESA	SURPRISE

LIST 13

	OTRA VEZ	AGAIN
	PLAYA	BEACH
	TIMBRE, CAMPANA	BELL
	BOTE, BARCA	BOAT
	AMBOS, LOS DOS	BOTH
	TARTA	CAKE
	EMPRESA	COMPANY
	RINCON, ESQUINA	CORNER
	TARDE (DESPUES DEL OSCURECER)	EVENING
	DEDO	FINGER
	MUEBLES	FURNITURE
	ABUELOS	GRANDPARENTS
	GRECIA	GREECE
	FELIZ, CONTENTO	HAPPY
	PESADO	HEAVY
	CASA, HOGAR	HOME
	ULTIMO	LAST
	CARTA	LETTER
	ALMUERZO, COMIDA	LUNCH
	AHORA	NOW
	PATATA	POTATO
	REDONDO	ROUND
	VARIOS	SEVERAL
	ZAPATOS	SHOES
	BLANDO, SUAVE	SOFT

BOLSA	BAG
CUARTO DE BAÑO	BATHROOM
HOMBRE DE NEGOCIOS	BUSINESSMAN
CENA	DINNER
TEMPRANO	EARLY
FABRICA	FACTORY
LEJOS	FAR
PIES	FEET
PLANO, LLANO	FLAT
COMIDA	FOOD
LIBRE	FREE
HOSPITAL	HOSPITAL
MAS TARDE	LATER
NOCHE	NIGHT
CARTERO	POSTMAN
RESULTADO	RESULT
AHORA MISMO	RIGHT NOW
SUELDO	SALARY
EXTRAÑO	STRANGE
LA POLICIA	THE POLICE
TIEMPO	TIME
HOY	TODAY
MAÑANA	TOMORROW
INVIERNO	WINTER
EQUIVOCADO	WRONG

LIST 15

	POR ENCIMA DE, SOBRE	ABOVE
	ACCION	ACTION
	TAMBIEN	ALSO
	PORQUE	BECAUSE
	FRONTERA	BORDER
	PUENTE	BRIDGE
	ROTO	BROKEN
	CADA	EACH
	ECONOMIA	ECONOMY
	TODOS LOS DIAS	EVERY DAY
	EXCEPTO	EXCEPT
	POR EJEMPLO	FOR EXAMPLE
	JARDIN	GARDEN
	GRUPO	GROUP
	INMEDIATAMENTE	IMMEDIATELY
	METODO	METHOD
	PARTE	PART
	LUGAR, SITIO	PLACE
	CAMISA	SHIRT
	ALGUNOS, ALGO DE	SOME
	VERANO	SUMMER
	LA PARTE SUPERIOR	THE TOP
	FUMAR	TO SMOKE
	URGENTE	URGENT
	UTIL	USEFUL

	Spanish	English
	EDAD	AGE
	LO ANTES POSIBLE	AS SOON AS POSSIBLE
	AYUDANTE	ASSISTANT
	ESPALDA	BACK
	TRANQUILO	CALM
	COMUN, CORRIENTE	COMMON
	ESFUERZO	EFFORT
	EVALUACION	EVALUATION
	AFORTUNADAMENTE	FORTUNATELY
	GENEROSO	GENEROUS
	POR LA TARDE	IN THE EVENING
	DENTRO, DENTRO DE	INSIDE
	INTERESANTE	INTERESTING
	PUNTO DE VISTA	POINT OF VIEW
	TAMAÑO, TALLA	SIZE
	ALLI, AHI	THERE
	ESTOS	THESE
	COSA	THING
	AQUELLOS	THOSE
	VENIR	TO COME
	BEBER	TO DRINK
	TENER	TO HAVE
	APRENDER	TO LEARN
	APRECIAR, GUSTARLE A UNO	TO LIKE
	MIRAR	TO LOOK AT

CUALQUIERA	ANYONE
CESTA	BASKET
CUERPO	BODY
TORO	BULL
COMPLETAMENTE	COMPLETELY
DICCIONARIO	DICTIONARY
ERROR	ERROR
CARO	EXPENSIVE
EXPLOTACION AGRICOLA, GRANJA	FARM
REGALO	GIFT
ABUELO	GRANDFATHER
SANO, SALUDABLE	HEALTHY
¿ COMO SE DICE ...?	HOW DO YOU SAY ...?
ENFERMO	ILL
DA IGUAL	IT DOESN'T MATTER
PRACTICO	PRACTICAL
PROBABLEMENTE	PROBABLY
RAPIDO	QUICK
RUTINA	ROUTINE
TRAJE	SUIT
LLAMAR	TO CALL
CERRAR	TO CLOSE
ESCUCHAR	TO LISTEN TO
BUSCAR	TO LOOK FOR
JUGAR	TO PLAY

	ACUERDO	AGREEMENT
	VALE, DE ACUERDO	ALL RIGHT
	SIEMPRE	ALWAYS
	CUANDO QUIERAS	ANYTIME
	DURACION	DURATION
	SOBRE TODO	ESPECIALLY
	EXACTAMENTE	EXACTLY
	DE VEZ EN CUANDO	FROM TIME TO TIME
	MEDIA HORA	HALF AN HOUR
	CERILLA	MATCH
	NOTA	NOTE
	NADA	NOTHING
	PAGO	PAYMENT
	FOTO	PHOTO
	DE COLOR ROSA	PINK
	ESPECIFICO	SPECIFIC
	TODAVIA	STILL
	EQUIPO	TEAM
	EL SOL	THE SUN
	PREGUNTAR	TO ASK
	CONDUCIR	TO DRIVE
	COMER	TO EAT
	AYUDAR	TO HELP
	SABER, CONOCER	TO KNOW
	MOJADO	WET

ATENCION	ATTENTION
ANTES, ANTES DE	BEFORE
DIARIO, DIARIAMENTE	DAILY
DECISION	DECISION
MITAD	HALF
A FAVOR DE	IN FAVOR OF
VAMONOS	LET'S GO
TODAVIA NO	NOT YET
A MENUDO	OFTEN
RAZON	REASON
ROSA	ROSE
SERVICIO	SERVICE
ESPECTACULO	SHOW
LADO	SIDE
EL MAR	THE SEA
CONTESTAR	TO ANSWER
COMPRAR	TO BUY
COSTAR	TO COST
DIBUJAR	TO DRAW
ENCONTRAR	TO FIND
OCURRIR	TO HAPPEN
OIR	TO HEAR
VIVIR	TO LIVE
MOVERSE, MUDARSE	TO MOVE
LEER	TO READ

	CASI	ALMOST
	A LO LARGO DE	ALONG
	POR DEBAJO DE	BELOW
	DENTISTA	DENTIST
	TAMPOCO	EITHER
	VACIO	EMPTY
	ENORME	ENORMOUS
	ESENCIAL	ESSENTIAL
	TODO EL MUNDO	EVERYBODY
	FUTURO	FUTURE
	MAS O MENOS	MORE OR LESS
	CASI	NEARLY
	NORTE	NORTH
	OFICINA DE CORREOS	POST OFFICE
	CALIDAD	QUALITY
	CIELO	SKY
	CANCION	SONG
	SONIDO	SOUND
	SUR	SOUTH
	PRIMAVERA	SPRING
	ASISTIR A	TO ATTEND
	ROMPER	TO BREAK
	CONTAR	TO COUNT
	DAR, ENTREGAR	TO GIVE
	RECIBIR	TO RECEIVE

LIST 21

	SOLO, EN SOLITARIO	ALONE
	ARTICULO	ARTICLE
	POR LO MENOS	AT LEAST
	AL LADO DE	BESIDE
	CAMARA (FOTOGRAFICA)	CAMERA
	DISCULPE	EXCUSE ME
	FINALMENTE, POR ULTIMO	FINALLY
	LLENO	FULL
	UBICACION	LOCATION
	OFICIAL	OFFICIAL
	LLUVIA	RAIN
	SEGUNDO	SECOND
	DESPUES, ENTONCES	THEN
	CREER	TO BELIEVE
	CUBRIR	TO COVER
	CORTAR	TO CUT
	SENTIR, PENSAR	TO FEEL
	CONSEGUIR, OBTENER	TO GET
	NECESITAR	TO NEED
	PRODUCIR	TO PRODUCE
	CERRAR	TO SHUT
	GASTAR, PASAR (TIEMPO)	TO SPEND
	ESTUDIAR	TO STUDY
	HABLAR, CHARLAR	TO TALK
	LLEVAR PUESTO	TO WEAR

	CUALQUIER COSA	ANYTHING
	APARTE DE	APART FROM
	ACTITUD	ATTITUDE
	CINTURON	BELT
	LIBRERIA	BOOKSTORE
	CASO	CASE
	POLLO	CHICKEN
	CHINO	CHINESE
	¡VENGA, VAMOS !	COME ON !
	MUERTO	DEAD
	SUFICIENTE	ENOUGH
	¡ DATE PRISA !	HURRY UP !
	INCOMPLETO	INCOMPLETE
	TAL VEZ	MAYBE
	PROPUESTA	PROPOSAL
	VENTAS	SALES
	EXITO	SUCCESS
	AÑADIR, SUMAR	TO ADD
	PEDIR	TO ASK FOR
	TENER PRISA	TO BE IN A HURRY
	DEPENDER DE	TO DEPEND ON
	LLENAR	TO FILL
	OFRECER	TO OFFER
	PREFERIR	TO PREFER
	TRABAJAR	TO WORK

LIST 23

	DISCUSION (ACALORADA)	ARGUMENT
	ASISTENCIA	ATTENDANCE
	OCUPADO	BUSY
	CLIMA, AMBIENTE	CLIMATE
	LOCO	CRAZY
	META	GOAL
	DE HECHO	IN FACT
	MEMORIA	MEMORY
	JAMAS, NUNCA	NEVER
	HORARIO, PROGRAMA	SCHEDULE
	PANTALLA	SCREEN
	EL TIEMPO (ATMOSFERICO)	THE WEATHER
	A TRAVES DE	THROUGH
	CONSTRUIR	TO BUILD
	EXIGIR	TO DEMAND
	ENFADARSE	TO GET ANGRY
	DESCANSAR	TO REST
	CORRER	TO RUN
	SONREIR	TO SMILE
	PENSAR	TO THINK
	INTENTAR	TO TRY TO
	PUEBLO, CIUDAD PEQUEÑA	TOWN
	MODO, FORMA, MANERA	WAY
	FIN DE SEMANA	WEEKEND
	PALABRA	WORD

	YA	ALREADY
	CUMPLEAÑOS	BIRTHDAY
	CUIDADOSO	CAREFUL
	HUEVO	EGG
	EUROPEO	EUROPEAN
	PELICULA	FILM
	GRACIOSO	FUNNY
	¿ CUANTO ?	HOW MUCH ...?
	EN GENERAL	IN GENERAL
	PIERNA	LEG
	MENSAJE	MESSAGE
	PROXIMO	NEXT
	PROPOSITO	PURPOSE
	TRISTE	SAD
	RECTO	STRAIGHT
	EL MISMO	THE SAME
	COMENZAR	TO BEGIN
	CONTINUAR	TO CONTINUE
	DESCRIBIR	TO DESCRIBE
	ESPERAR, PREVER	TO EXPECT
	EXPLICAR	TO EXPLAIN
	PREPARAR	TO PREPARE
	VER	TO SEE
	RESOLVER	TO SOLVE
	PONERSE DE PIE	TO STAND UP

LIST 25

	CANTIDAD, IMPORTE	AMOUNT
	CERCA DE	CLOSE TO
	REFERENTE A	CONCERNING
	CORTINA	CURTAIN
	PROFUNDO	DEEP
	DEPARTAMENTO	DEPARTMENT
	EFICAZ	EFFECTIVE
	TODO EL MUNDO	EVERYONE
	EJERCICIO	EXERCISE
	EXPERTO	EXPERT
	NIETO	GRANDSON
	GRIEGO	GREEK
	CARRETERA, AUTOVIA	HIGHWAY
	ESPERANZA	HOPE
	INFLACION	INFLATION
	COMO, AL IGUAL QUE	LIKE
	PODER, POTENCIA	POWER
	PRIORIDAD	PRIORITY
	LLEGAR	TO ARRIVE
	OLVIDAR	TO FORGET
	CRECER	TO GROW
	AUMENTAR	TO INCREASE
	DURAR	TO LAST
	AMAR, QUERER	TO LOVE
	EMPUJAR	TO PUSH

	UNA OFERTA	AN OFFER
	OPORTUNIDAD, POSIBILIDAD	CHANCE
	DISTANCIA	DISTANCE
	GENERALMENTE	GENERALLY
	REAL, AUTENTICO	REAL
	SENCILLO	SIMPLE
	QUEMAR, ARDER	TO BURN
	CAMBIAR	TO CHANGE
	DECIDIR	TO DECIDE
	DEFENDER	TO DEFEND
	TERMINAR	TO FINISH
	VOLAR	TO FLY
	LLEGAR A	TO GET TO
	ESPERAR (CON ILUSION)	TO HOPE
	MARCHARSE	TO LEAVE
	PERDER	TO LOSE
	PAGAR	TO PAY
	PROMETER	TO PROMISE
	ALQUILAR	TO RENT
	OLER	TO SMELL
	VISITAR	TO VISIT
	VACACIONES	VACATION
	VERDURAS	VEGETABLES
	PUEBLO PEQUEÑO	VILLAGE
	VOCABULARIO	VOCABULARY

LIST 27

	DE TODOS MODOS	ANYWAY
	CONSECUENCIAS	CONSEQUENCES
	TODO	EVERYTHING
	EXCELENTE	EXCELLENT
	JUSTO	FAIR
	SIN EMBARGO	HOWEVER
	NADIE	NOBODY
	PROFESION	PROFESSION
	ALGUN DIA	SOMEDAY
	ALGUIEN	SOMEONE
	TIENDA, ALMACEN	STORE
	SUPERMERCADO	SUPERMARKET
	SEGURO	SURE
	DULCE	SWEET
	EL MUNDO	THE WORLD
	ACEPTAR	TO ACCEPT
	ATACAR	TO ATTACK
	ATRAER	TO ATTRACT
	ELEGIR	TO CHOOSE
	COCINAR, COCER	TO COOK
	SEGUIR	TO FOLLOW
	MEJORAR	TO IMPROVE
	INCLUIR	TO INCLUDE
	JUBILARSE	TO RETIRE
	PARAR, DETENER	TO STOP

CUALQUIERA	ANYBODY
ADEMAS, ADEMAS DE	BESIDES
DEFECTO	DEFECT
CORAZON	HEART
AGUJERO	HOLE
CONOCIMIENTOS	KNOWLEDGE
TIERRA	LAND
PUNTUAL	ON TIME
JUBILACION	RETIREMENT
TEMPORADA, ESTACION (DE AÑO)	SEASON
DISCURSO	SPEECH
BILLETE	TICKET
TENER SUERTE	TO BE LUCKY
COMPARAR	TO COMPARE
MORIR	TO DIE
GANAR (TRABAJANDO)	TO EARN
CAER	TO FALL
CONOCER POR VEZ PRIMERA	TO MEET
TIRAR (CONTRARIO DE EMPUJAR)	TO PULL
RECOMENDAR	TO RECOMMEND
REVISAR, REPASAR	TO REVIEW
VIAJAR	TO TRAVEL
ESTA NOCHE	TONIGHT
TRAFICO	TRAFFIC
VIAJE	TRIP

	EN CUALQUIER SITIO	ANYPLACE
	PROMEDIO	AVERAGE
	EQUILIBRIO	BALANCE
	FACTURA	BILL
	POTENTE, PODEROSO	POWERFUL
	REINA	QUEEN
	RAPIDAMENTE	QUICKLY
	SATISFECHO	SATISFIED
	ESTILO	STYLE
	ESTAR DE ACUERDO CON	TO AGREE WITH
	LIMPIAR	TO CLEAN
	CONSIDERAR	TO CONSIDER
	DISFRUTAR DE	TO ENJOY
	IR A CASA	TO GO HOME
	LLOVER	TO RAIN
	REDUCIR	TO REDUCE
	ROBAR	TO STEAL
	LANZAR, ARROJAR	TO THROW
	ENTENDER	TO UNDERSTAND
	UTILIZAR	TO USE
	CAMION	TRUCK
	FEO	UGLY
	NORMALMENTE	USUALLY
	VALOR	VALUE
	ENTERO	WHOLE

	EN CUALQUIER SITIO	ANYWHERE
	DETALLE	DETAIL
	FACILMENTE	EASILY
	ACONTECIMIENTO	EVENT
	FRACASO	FAILURE
	SALUD	HEALTH
	GERENTE, DIRECTOR	MANAGER
	PRESION	PRESSURE
	REFERENTE A	REGARDING
	SEGURIDAD (FISICA)	SAFETY
	DE EXITO, EXITOSO	SUCCESSFUL
	EL MEJOR	THE BEST
	PERMITIR	TO ALLOW
	TENER MIEDO DE	TO BE AFRAID OF
	SER ABURRIDO	TO BE BORING
	COGER	TO CATCH
	LLORAR	TO CRY
	VACIAR	TO EMPTY
	HACER	TO MAKE
	PLANEAR, PLANIFICAR	TO PLAN
	AHORRAR	TO SAVE
	DECIR	TO SAY
	MOSTRAR, ENSEÑAR	TO SHOW
	LAVAR	TO WASH
	OESTE	WEST

LIST 31

	SENTIDO COMUN	COMMON SENSE
	PRIMO, PRIMA	COUSIN
	ENTREGA	DELIVERY
	DEBIDO A	DUE TO
	EXPLICACION	EXPLANATION
	AGRICULTOR	FARMER
	EXTRANJERO (SUSTANTIVO)	FOREIGNER
	IMPRESO, FORMULARIO	FORM
	VAGO, PEREZOSO	LAZY
	NATURALEZA	NATURE
	NADIE	NO ONE
	NORMALMENTE	NORMALLY
	RESPETO	RESPECT
	ETAPA	STAGE
	TRAER	TO BRING
	CRUZAR	TO CROSS
	ESCAPAR	TO ESCAPE
	INVITAR	TO INVITE
	VENDER	TO SELL
	ESTAR SENTADO	TO SIT
	NEVAR	TO SNOW
	HABLAR	TO SPEAK
	SORPRENDER	TO SURPRISE
	DESEAR, QUERER	TO WANT
	HACIA ARRIBA	UP

DE CUALQUIER MODO	ANYHOW
ASPECTO	ASPECT
NEGOCIO	BUSINESS
COMPARACION	COMPARISON
RETRASO	DELAY
INCLUSO, AUN	EVEN
VIDA	LIFE
POBLACION	POPULATION
ACTUAR	TO ACT
ESTAR ABURRIDO	TO BE BORED
PERTENECER A	TO BELONG TO
PONERSE EN CONTACTO CON	TO CONTACT
SOÑAR	TO DREAM
ESTABLECER	TO ESTABLISH
LUCHAR, PELEAR	TO FIGHT
ALCANZAR	TO REACH
SERVIR	TO SERVE
ESTAR DE PIE	TO STAND
ENSEÑAR	TO TEACH
DECIR, CONTAR	TO TELL
ANDAR	TO WALK
ESCRIBIR	TO WRITE
HASTA	UNTIL
¿ QUE PASA ?	WHAT'S THE MATTER ?
MADERA	WOOD

LIST 33

	Spanish	English
	AL PRINCIPIO	AT FIRST
	COMPARADO CON	COMPARED TO / WITH
	ALGO FRIO, FRESCO	COOL
	DURANTE	DURING
	ENFASIS	EMPHASIS
	SOBRE	ENVELOPE
	EN TODAS PARTES	EVERYWHERE
	DIVERTIDO	FUN
	NIETA	GRANDDAUGHTER
	HIELO	ICE
	ADEMAS DE	IN ADDITION TO
	PEDAZO, TROZO	PIECE
	EDUCADO	POLITE
	RIESGO	RISK
	HASTA AHORA	SO FAR
	ESTABLE	STABLE
	CONVERTIRSE EN, LLEGAR A SER	TO BECOME
	LLEVAR	TO CARRY
	COPIAR	TO COPY
	BAILAR	TO DANCE
	ESTAR EN DESACUERDO	TO DISAGREE
	LEVANTARSE	TO GET UP
	ODIAR	TO HATE
	¿ QUE QUIERES DECIR ?	WHAT DO YOU MEAN ?
	PREOCUPADO	WORRIED

	FONDO, PARTE INFERIOR	BOTTOM
	CIRCUNSTANCIAS	CIRCUMSTANCES
	CASUALIDAD	COINCIDENCE
	CURSO	COURSE
	SENTIMIENTOS	FEELINGS
	CIFRAS	FIGURES
	EXTRANJERO (ADJETIVO)	FOREIGN
	AGRADABLE	PLEASANT
	SEGURO (LIBRE DE PELIGRO)	SAFE
	DELGADO	THIN
	COMPROBAR	TO CHECK
	CONVERSAR SOBRE UN TEMA	TO DISCUSS
	DIVIDIR	TO DIVIDE
	NOTAR	TO NOTICE
	PROGRESAR	TO PROGRESS
	SUSTITUIR	TO REPLACE
	EMPEZAR	TO START
	QUEDARSE, PERMANECER	TO STAY
	NADAR	TO SWIM
	ESCRIBIR A MAQUINA	TO TYPE
	ESPERAR	TO WAIT
	VERDADERO, VERDAD	TRUE
	VISTA	VIEW
	¿ QUE CLASE DE ...?	WHAT KIND OF ..?
	MARAVILLOSO	WONDERFUL

SEGUN	ACCORDING TO
ANUNCIO (EN PRENSA)	ADVERTISEMENT
CONTRA	AGAINST
DORMIDO	ASLEEP
MEJOR QUE	BETTER THAN
CEPILLO	BRUSH
COCINERO	COOK
POCOS	FEW
ABUELA	GRANDMOTHER
UVAS	GRAPES
HELADO	ICE CREAM
IMPOSIBLE	IMPOSSIBLE
EN VEZ DE	INSTEAD OF
ISLA	ISLAND
MAS QUE	MORE THAN
CUELLO	NECK
NINGUNO	NONE
ESTAR DE ACUERDO	TO AGREE
COLGAR	TO HANG
SUJETAR, SOSTENER	TO HOLD
SALTAR	TO JUMP
GUARDAR, MANTENER	TO KEEP
PINTAR	TO PAINT
ELEGIR	TO PICK
VER, OBSERVAR	TO WATCH

	EQUIPAJE	BAGGAGE
	MENOS QUE	LESS THAN
	PERDEDOR	LOSER
	QUIZAS	PERHAPS
	BASTANTE	QUITE
	LENTAMENTE	SLOWLY
	ASI QUE, POR TANTO	SO
	ALGUIEN	SOMEBODY
	ALGO	SOMETHING
	A VECES	SOMETIMES
	SELLO	STAMP
	PISCINA	SWIMMING POOL
	IR DE COMPRAS	TO GO SHOPPING
	DARSE PRISA	TO HURRY
	ENVIAR	TO SEND
	CANTAR	TO SING
	SENTARSE	TO SIT DOWN
	DORMIR	TO SLEEP
	LLEVAR, TOMAR	TO TAKE
	INTENTAR	TO TRY
	DESPERTARSE	TO WAKE UP
	GANAR	TO WIN
	CALENTITO	WARM
	DEBIL	WEAK
	GANADOR	WINNER

Vocabulary booklet 2

NIVEL PRINCIPIANTE

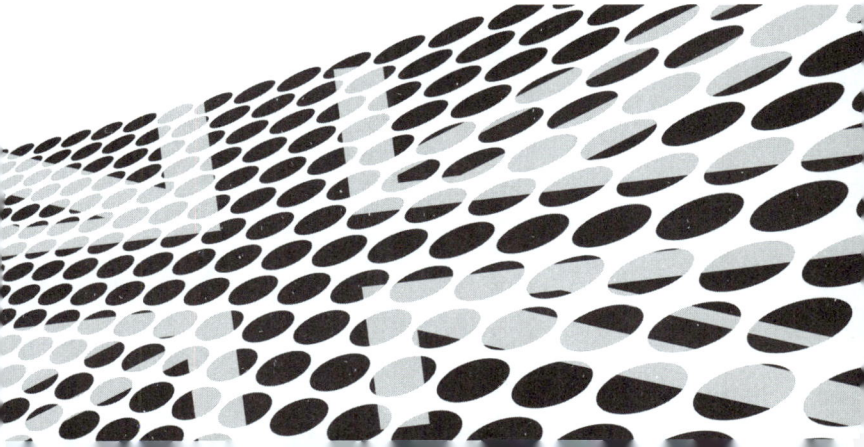

LIST 1

	ACEPTABLE	ACCEPTABLE
	ALREDEDOR DE	AROUND
	DESPIERTO	AWAKE
	BRASILEÑO	BRAZILIAN
	AMPLIO	BROAD
	CON CUIDADO	CAREFULLY
	DOBLE	DOUBLE
	DURACION	DURATION
	FACILMENTE	EASILY
	ENFASIS	EMPHASIS
	REGALO	GIFT
	CRECIMIENTO	GROWTH
	DELANTE DE	IN FRONT OF
	INCOMPLETO	INCOMPLETE
	RUIDO	NOISE
	ENFERMO	SICK
	LETRERO	SIGN
	LENTO	SLOW
	HASTA AHORA	SO FAR
	BLANDO, SUAVE	SOFT
	AJUSTAR	TO ADJUST
	MOLESTAR	TO BOTHER
	LLEVAR	TO CARRY
	CONGELAR	TO FREEZE
	PERDER	TO LOSE

	Spanish	English
	ACCESO	ACCESS
	VENTAJA	ADVANTAGE
	POR DELANTE	AHEAD
	TERRIBLEMENTE	AWFULLY
	POR DEBAJO DE	BELOW
	CUÑADO	BROTHER-IN-LAW
	VIDA PROFESIONAL	CAREER
	EN TODAS PARTES	EVERYWHERE
	SENTIMIENTOS	FEELINGS
	PREVISION	FORECAST
	EXTRANJERO	FOREIGNER
	SALUD	HEALTH
	COLINA	HILL
	IMAGEN	IMAGE
	IMPRESIONANTE	IMPRESSIVE
	EN VEZ DE	INSTEAD OF
	CORDERO	LAMB
	TAL VEZ	MAYBE
	EDUCADO	POLITE
	CREAR	TO CREATE
	DESTRUIR	TO DESTROY
	MANEJAR	TO HANDLE
	IMAGINAR	TO IMAGINE
	JUICIO, PROCESO JUDICIAL	TRIAL
	INJUSTO	UNFAIR

LIST 3

A / EN EL EXTRANJERO	ABROAD
CUENTA	ACCOUNT
PROMEDIO	AVERAGE
CASUALIDAD	COINCIDENCE
FORMACION ACADEMICA	EDUCATION
PLANO, LLANO	FLAT
BIBLIOTECA	LIBRARY
EN CAMBIO	ON THE OTHER HAND
PUNTO DE VISTA	POINT OF VIEW
CENTRO DE COMPRAS	SHOPPING CENTER
ACEPTAR	TO ACCEPT
TENER PRISA	TO BE IN A HURRY
CAUSAR	TO CAUSE
LLENAR	TO FILL
REPARAR, ARREGLAR	TO FIX
PERDONAR	TO FORGIVE
LLEGAR A	TO GET TO
OIR	TO HEAR
SUJETAR, SOSTENER	TO HOLD
MEJORAR	TO IMPROVE
INCLUIR	TO INCLUDE
SOSPECHAR	TO SUSPECT
LANZAR, ARROJAR	TO THROW
ENCENDER	TO TURN ON
SIN DUDA	WITHOUT A DOUBT

	UNA NECESIDAD	A NEED
	ACOSTUMBRADO A	ACCUSTOMED TO
	EN VOZ ALTA	ALOUD
	CITA	APPOINTMENT
	EQUILIBRIO	BALANCE
	DESGLOSE	BREAKDOWN
	ROPA	CLOTHES
	CRITERIOS	CRITERIA
	MESA DE TRABAJO	DESK
	MOTOR	ENGINE
	INCLUSO, AUN	EVEN
	FINALMENTE, POR ULTIMO	FINALLY
	DIRECTRICES	GUIDELINES
	IDIOMA	LANGUAGE
	ENFADADO	MAD
	ESTRECHO	NARROW
	POLITICA (DE EMPRESA)	POLICY
	RAZON	REASON
	SATISFECHO	SATISFIED
	SIMPLEMENTE	SIMPLY
	PASO	STEP
	IMPUESTOS	TAXES
	PERMITIRSE EL LUJO DE	TO AFFORD
	SER ABURRIDO	TO BE BORING
	EXISTIR	TO EXIST

LIST 5

1	HABILIDAD, PERICIA	ABILITY
2	AVANZADO	ADVANCED
3	TAMBIEN	ALSO
4	APROBACIÓN	APPROVAL
5	VIAJE DE NEGOCIOS	BUSINESS TRIP
6	COMPARADO CON	COMPARED TO / WITH
7	DIARIO, DIARIAMENTE	DAILY
8	DEBIDO A	DUE TO
9	ENTERO	ENTIRE
10	EXCEPTO	EXCEPT
11	DE VEZ EN CUANDO	FROM TIME TO TIME
12	SIN EMBARGO	HOWEVER
13	INCOMPETENTE	INCOMPETENT
14	¿ PUEDO HABLAR CON ...?	MAY I SPEAK TO ... ?
15	MECANICO	MECHANIC
16	PAGO	PAYMENT
17	SILENCIOSO	QUIET
18	MAL EDUCADO	RUDE
19	DE ALGUNA MANERA	SOMEHOW
20	ESTABLE	STABLE
21	SORPRESA	SURPRISE
22	EL PRINCIPIO	THE BEGINNING
23	ADOPTAR	TO ADOPT
24	ESTAR ABURRIDO	TO BE BORED
25	BAJAR, DESCENDER	TO GO DOWN

ABSOLUTAMENTE	ABSOLUTELY
PUBLICIDAD	ADVERTISING
AUNQUE	ALTHOUGH
ENTRE	AMONG
TAN PRONTO COMO, EN CUANTO	AS SOON AS
AL LADO DE	BESIDE
CAPACIDAD	CAPACITY
CONFIADO	CONFIDENT
DEFECTUOSO	DEFECTIVE
IGUAL	EQUAL
SOBRE TODO	ESPECIALLY
ARCHIVO, EXPEDIENTE	FILE
SANO, SALUDABLE	HEALTHY
EN DETALLE	IN DETAIL
INFLACION	INFLATION
VAMONOS	LET'S GO
MUSEO	MUSEUM
RUIDOSO	NOISY
PROBABLEMENTE	PROBABLY
JUBILACION	RETIREMENT
TAMAÑO, TALLA	SIZE
ESCALERAS	STAIRS
TRAJE	SUIT
TITULO	TITLE
ESCONDER, OCULTAR	TO HIDE

	SEGUN	ACCORDING TO
	ASUNTO	AFFAIR
	ANALISIS	ANALYSIS
	AYUDANTE	ASSISTANT
	CIEGO	BLIND
	CLARO, TRANSPARENTE	CLEAR
	CRITICA	CRITICISM
	DESVENTAJA	DISADVANTAGE
	EXAMEN	EXAM
	EJEMPLO	EXAMPLE
	FRUSTRADO	FRUSTRATED
	ME TRAE SIN CUIDADO	I DON'T CARE
	CELOSO	JEALOUS
	LA MAYORIA DE	MOST
	SOBRINA	NIECE
	POTENTE, PODEROSO	POWERFUL
	RECURSOS	RESOURCES
	SIMILAR	SIMILAR
	DE REPENTE	SUDDENLY
	CENA	SUPPER
	PROPINA	TIP
	TENER MIEDO DE	TO BE AFRAID OF
	COMPRAR	TO BUY
	CONVENCER	TO CONVINCE
	POSEER	TO OWN

	REAL	ACTUAL
	INQUIETO, AMBICIOSO	AMBITIOUS
	OTRO	ANOTHER
	AMBIENTE, ATMOSFERA	ATMOSPHERE
	AMBOS, LOS DOS	BOTH
	COMUN, CORRIENTE	COMMON
	PELIGROSO	DANGEROUS
	EFICAZ	EFFECTIVE
	JUSTO	FAIR
	MAS LEJOS	FARTHER
	DURO	HARD
	A FAVOR DE	IN FAVOR OF
	ALTO (UN RUIDO)	LOUD
	HOY EN DIA	NOWADAYS
	PORCENTAJE	PERCENTAGE
	LISTO, PREPARADO	READY
	TEMPORADA	SEASON
	FUERTE	STRONG
	LLAMADA TELEFONICA	TELEPHONE CALL
	GRUESO, ESPESO	THICK
	ASISTIR A	TO ATTEND
	CONSTRUIR	TO BUILD
	CONTINUAR	TO CONTINUE
	DUDAR	TO DOUBT
	PARECER	TO SEEM

	EN REALIDAD	ACTUALLY
	ANUAL	ANNUAL
	CUALQUIERA	ANYONE
	ACTITUD	ATTITUDE
	EDIFICIO	BUILDING
	QUEJA	COMPLAINT
	DEFECTO	DEFECT
	ACONTECIMIENTO	EVENT
	SUELTO, FLUIDO (HABLANDO)	FLUENT
	AFORTUNADAMENTE	FORTUNATELY
	ENORME	HUGE
	LLAVE, CLAVE	KEY
	NERVIOSO	NERVOUS
	DUEÑO	OWNER
	BENEFICIOS (ECONOMICOS)	PROFITS
	RUTINA	ROUTINE
	TODAVIA	STILL
	EL SUELO	THE GROUND
	LO CONTRARIO DE	THE OPPOSITE OF
	PEDIR	TO ASK FOR
	ROMPER EL HIELO	TO BREAK THE ICE
	CONSULTAR CON	TO CONSULT
	DISTRIBUIR	TO DISTRIBUTE
	SEGUIR	TO FOLLOW
	PREOCUPARSE	TO WORRY

	Spanish	English
	SEÑAS, DIRECCION	ADDRESS
	HORMIGA	ANT
	CUALQUIER COSA	ANYTHING
	HERMOSO	BEAUTIFUL
	POR CIERTO, A PROPOSITO	BY THE WAY
	CONSECUENCIAS	CONSEQUENCES
	DEDICADO A	DEVOTED TO
	EXCEPCION	EXCEPTION
	FRECUENTE	FREQUENT
	GESTO, DETALLE	GESTURE
	RESPONSABLE DE	IN CHARGE OF
	AFORTUNADO	LUCKY
	PARRAFO	PARAGRAPH
	FASE	PHASE
	INFORME	REPORT
	DESDE CUANDO ...	SINCE WHEN ...
	SISTEMA	SYSTEM
	CANSADO	TIRED
	APARECER	TO APPEAR
	PERTENECER A	TO BELONG TO
	CONFIRMAR	TO CONFIRM
	ESTAR EN DESACUERDO	TO DISAGREE
	AVERIGUAR, ENTERARSE	TO FIND OUT
	IDENTIFICAR	TO IDENTIFY
	TORRE	TOWER

	ADECUADO	ADEQUATE
	DE TODOS MODOS	ANYWAY
	ASPECTO, APARIENCIA	APPEARANCE
	DETRAS DE	BEHIND
	TECHO	CEILING
	MULTITUD, MUCHEDUMBRE	CROWD
	BARATO	ECONOMICAL
	CIFRAS	FIGURES
	FRESCO	FRESH
	DIA FESTIVO	HOLIDAY
	NO TIENE SENTIDO	IT DOESN'T MAKE SENSE
	OLVIDALO	NEVER MIND
	TUBO, TUBERIA	PIPE
	PROPOSITO	PURPOSE
	HORARIO, PROGRAMA	SCHEDULE
	TEMA	SUBJECT
	AVANZAR	TO ADVANCE
	PEDIR PERDON	TO APOLOGIZE
	ESTAR SEGURO DE	TO BE SURE OF
	ACLARAR	TO CLEAR UP
	DESARROLLAR	TO DEVELOP
	RELLENAR (IMPRESOS)	TO FILL OUT
	DARSE PRISA	TO HURRY
	ORGANIZAR	TO ORGANIZE
	VOZ	VOICE

ANUNCIO (DE PRENSA)	ADVERTISEMENT
APARTE DE	APART FROM
LLEGADA	ARRIVAL
BENEFICIOSO	BENEFICIAL
CLIMA, AMBIENTE	CLIMATE
FECHA	DATE
ESENCIAL	ESSENTIAL
LIBREMENTE	FREELY
CONTENTO	GLAD
INMEDIATAMENTE	IMMEDIATELY
UBICACION	LOCATION
LLAMADA TELEFONICA	PHONE CALL
IMPRESORA	PRINTER
RESPETABLE	RESPECTABLE
AFIRMACION	STATEMENT
LA PARTE SUPERIOR	THE TOP
EVITAR	TO AVOID
EQUILIBRAR	TO BALANCE
COGER	TO CATCH
ENTREGAR	TO DELIVER
SENTIR, PENSAR	TO FEEL
PEGAR, GOLPEAR	TO HIT
OFRECER	TO OFFER
RECHAZAR	TO REJECT
MIENTRAS, MIENTRAS QUE	WHILE

	POR ENCIMA DE, SOBRE	ABOVE
	CONSEJO, ASESORAMIENTO	ADVICE
	ENFOQUE, PLANTEAMIENTO	APPROACH
	AUTOR	AUTHOR
	ENTRE	BETWEEN
	SENTIDO COMUN	COMMON SENSE
	RETRASO	DELAY
	EXACTAMENTE	EXACTLY
	META	GOAL
	GOBIERNO	GOVERNMENT
	INGRESOS	INCOME
	NATURALEZA	NATURE
	PROHIBIDO	PROHIBITED
	CALIDAD	QUALITY
	FRASE	SENTENCE
	SUPERFICIE	SURFACE
	APROBAR	TO APPROVE
	SACAR (UN TEMA)	TO BRING UP
	TREPAR, SUBIR	TO CLIMB
	TRATAR CON	TO DEAL WITH
	EXCLUIR	TO EXCLUDE
	DIVERTIRSE, PASARLO BIEN	TO HAVE A GOOD TIME
	MEZCLAR	TO MIX
	ARREPENTIRSE	TO REGRET
	FIRMAR	TO SIGN

	Spanish	English
1	MIEDOSO, TEMEROSO	AFRAID
2	APROXIMADAMENTE	APPROXIMATELY
3	HORRIBLE	AWFUL
4	FRONTERA	BORDER
5	COMPLETAMENTE	COMPLETELY
6	DIFICULTAD	DIFFICULTY
7	FRACASO	FAILURE
8	HIERBA, CESPED	GRASS
9	PERDIDO, SIN ESPERANZA	HOPELESS
10	MAS TARDE	LATER
11	QUIZAS	PERHAPS
12	TRIMESTRE	QUARTER
13	RESULTADO	RESULT
14	RECTO	STRAIGHT
15	A TRAVES DE	THROUGH
16	CONVERTIRSE EN, LLEGAR A SER	TO BECOME
17	CONSISTIR EN	TO CONSIST OF
18	VACIAR	TO EMPTY
19	CAERSE	TO FALL DOWN
20	EMPEORARSE	TO GET WORSE
21	DIRIGIR	TO MANAGE
22	PRONUNCIAR	TO PRONOUNCE
23	REDUCIR	TO REDUCE
24	CERRAR	TO SHUT
25	INTENTAR	TO TRY TO

	Spanish	English
	DESPUES	AFTERWARDS
	COMO SI	AS IF
	HACIA ATRAS	BACKWARD
	BREVE	BRIEF
	CONSTANTEMENTE	CONSTANTLY
	ECONOMIA	ECONOMY
	IMPRESO, FORMULARIO	FORM
	JUDIAS VERDES	GREEN BEANS
	ADEMAS DE	IN ADDITION TO
	METODO	METHOD
	PROPUESTA	PROPOSAL
	RECIENTEMENTE	RECENTLY
	VARIOS	SEVERAL
	TRABAJO EN EQUIPO	TEAMWORK
	ATACAR	TO ATTACK
	CAMBIAR DE TEMA	TO CHANGE THE SUBJECT
	MORIR	TO DIE
	BORRAR	TO ERASE
	APAÑARSE, SALIR DEL PASO	TO GET BY
	ENTRAR EN	TO GO INTO
	LOCALIZAR	TO LOCATE
	DARSE CUENTA DE	TO REALIZE
	FIJAR, ESTABLECER	TO SET
	CONFIAR EN, FIARSE DE	TO TRUST
	URGENTE	URGENT

	Spanish	English
	COMO DE COSTUMBRE	AS USUAL
	BANQUERO	BANKER
	HOMBRE DE NEGOCIOS	BUSINESSMAN
	ABARROTADO	CROWDED
	EVALUACION	EVALUATION
	GENEROSO	GENEROUS
	TIPO, INDIVIDUO	GUY
	LA FELICIDAD	HAPPINESS
	INTERESADO EN	INTERESTED IN
	A PROPOSITO	ON PURPOSE
	REQUISITOS	REQUIREMENTS
	AFILADO, AGUDO	SHARP
	PLATA	SILVER
	ESTAR DE ACUERDO CON	TO AGREE WITH
	ROMPER	TO BREAK
	DISMINUIR	TO DECREASE
	ARCHIVAR	TO FILE
	DURAR	TO LAST
	SIGNIFICAR, QUERER DECIR	TO MEAN
	PRACTICAR	TO PRACTICE
	PROGRAMAR	TO SCHEDULE
	TIRAR (A LA BASURA)	TO THROW AWAY
	JUGUETE	TOY
	ACTUALIZADO	UP TO DATE
	RUEDA	WHEEL

	CONTRA, EN CONTRA DE	AGAINST
	LO ANTES POSIBLE	AS SOON AS POSSIBLE
	SOTANO	BASEMENT
	BASE, FUNDAMENTO	BASIS
	ROTO	BROKEN
	COMODO, OPORTUNO	CONVENIENT
	ESFUERZO	EFFORT
	LIBRE	FREE
	AMA DE CASA	HOUSEWIFE
	EN TODO CASO	IN ANY CASE
	MENTE	MIND
	ORGULLOSO	PROUD
	TIMIDO	SHY
	JABON	SOAP
	ESO ES, EN EFECTO	THAT'S RIGHT
	ATRAER	TO ATTRACT
	CONVERSAR (SOBRE UN TEMA)	TO DISCUSS
	PONERSE NERVIOSO	TO GET NERVOUS
	BUSCAR	TO LOOK FOR
	ADELANTAR, PASAR	TO PASS
	RECONOCER	TO RECOGNIZE
	GRITAR	TO SHOUT
	VIAJAR	TO TRAVEL
	GIRAR, TORCER	TO TURN
	UTIL	USEFUL

1	EDAD	AGE
2	CUANDO QUIERAS	ANYTIME
3	JUDIAS	BEANS
4	PORQUE	BECAUSE
5	TRANQUILO	CALM
6	REFERENTE A	CONCERNING
7	ENTREGA	DELIVERY
8	TODOS LOS DIAS	EVERYDAY
9	POR EJEMPLO	FOR EXAMPLE
10	¿ COMO SE DICE ...?	HOW DO YOU SAY ...?
11	ENFERMEDAD	ILLNESS
12	DA IGUAL	IT DOESN'T MATTER
13	MEZCLA	MIXTURE
14	PRACTICO	PRACTICAL
15	AHORA MISMO	RIGHT NOW
16	ESPECIFICO	SPECIFIC
17	CUADRADO	SQUARE
18	SIMBOLO	SYMBOL
19	ANALIZAR	TO ANALYZE
20	VALER	TO BE WORTH
21	ELEGIR	TO CHOOSE
22	DEFINIR	TO DEFINE
23	EVALUAR	TO EVALUATE
24	SUBIR, ASCENDER	TO GO UP
25	HACIA	TOWARD

1	ACUERDO	AGREEMENT
2	DISCUSION (ACALORADA)	ARGUMENT
3	OSO	BEAR
4	CUERPO	BODY
5	COMPARACION	COMPARISON
6	RESPONSABLE	DEPENDABLE
7	CARO	EXPENSIVE
8	PESADO	HEAVY
9	INTERESANTE	INTERESTING
10	IRLANDES	IRISH
11	TODAVIA NO	NOT YET
12	TASA	RATE
13	FIRMA	SIGNATURE
14	TAL	SUCH
15	EQUIPO	TEAM
16	ARREGLAR, ORGANIZAR	TO ARRANGE
17	PREGUNTAR	TO ASK
18	LLAMAR	TO CALL
19	DECIDIR	TO DECIDE
20	EXPLICAR	TO EXPLAIN
21	AYUDAR	TO HELP
22	TRABAR CONOCIMIENTO	TO MEET
23	RECOMENDAR	TO RECOMMEND
24	ASUSTAR	TO SCARE
25	SANDIA	WATERMELON

▪	VALE, DE ACUERDO	ALL RIGHT
▪	ATENCION	ATTENTION
▪	BELGA	BELGIAN
▪	CIRCUNSTANCIAS	CIRCUMSTANCES
▪	EXIGENTE	DEMANDING
▪	INCENDIO, FUEGO	FIRE
▪	MEJORA	IMPROVEMENT
▪	CUCHILLO	KNIFE
▪	CASI	NEARLY
10	RECOMENDACION	RECOMMENDATION
11	ESTRATEGIA	STRATEGY
12	GUIA TELEFONICA	TELEPHONE BOOK
13	CONTESTAR	TO ANSWER
14	VOLVER A TELEFONEAR	TO CALL BACK
15	DIBUJAR	TO DRAW
16	TERMINAR	TO END
17	ENCONTRAR	TO FIND
18	ENRIQUECERSE	TO GET RICH
19	NOTAR	TO NOTICE
20	SUSTITUIR	TO REPLACE
21	AFIRMAR	TO STATE
22	JUGUETES	TOYS
23	MOJADO	WET
24	¿ LE IMPORTARIA ...?	WOULD YOU MIND ...?
25	ESCRITOR	WRITER

	Spanish	English
1	CASI	ALMOST
2	POR LO MENOS	AT LEAST
3	BANCO (PARA SENTARSE)	BENCH
4	CAPAZ DE	CAPABLE OF
5	ACTUAL	CURRENT
6	TODO EL MUNDO	EVERYBODY
7	GIGANTE	GIANT
8	IMPUESTO SOBRE LA RENTA	INCOME TAX
9	NIVEL	LEVEL
10	AL CONTRARIO	ON THE CONTRARY
11	REFERENTE A	REGARDING
12	ESTADISTICAS	STATISTICS
13	EL CORREO	THE MAIL
14	PENSAMIENTOS	THOUGHTS
15	CREER	TO BELIEVE
16	CUBRIR	TO COVER
17	AMPLIAR	TO EXPAND
18	HACERSE MAYOR	TO GROW UP
19	AUMENTAR	TO INCREASE
20	PRODUCIR	TO PRODUCE
21	PEDIR	TO REQUEST
22	GASTAR, PASAR (TIEMPO)	TO SPEND
23	LLEVAR PUESTO	TO WEAR
24	VALIOSO	VALUABLE
25	VIENTO	WIND

1	SOLO, EN SOLITARIO	ALONE
2	ADECUADO, APROPIADO	APPROPRIATE
3	BELGICA	BELGIUM
4	MEJOR QUE	BETTER THAN
5	VENGA, VAMOS	COME ON !
6	MUERTO	DEAD
7	SUFICIENTE	ENOUGH
8	COMIDA	FOOD
9	¡ DATE PRISA !	HURRY UP !
10	ULTIMAMENTE	LATELY
11	PERDIDO	LOST
12	PRINCIPAL	MAIN
13	POR SUPUESTO	OF COURSE
14	PROPIEDAD	PROPERTY
15	BASTANTES	QUITE A FEW
16	VENTAS	SALES
17	EXITO	SUCCESS
18	LADRON	THIEF
19	AÑADIR, SUMAR	TO ADD
20	SER OPTIMISTA	TO BE OPTIMISTIC
21	COMENTAR	TO COMMENT ON
22	DEPENDER DE	TO DEPEND ON
23	TENER GANAS DE	TO FEEL LIKE
24	CONTRATAR (A EMPLEADOS)	TO HIRE
25	TOMAR UNA DECISION	TO MAKE A DECISION

	A LO LARGO DE	ALONG
	ASISTENCIA	ATTENDANCE
	DEBAJO DE	BENEATH
	OCUPADO	BUSY
	LOCO	CRAZY
	ENORME	ENORMOUS
	LLENO	FULL
	DE HECHO	IN FACT
	MEMORIA	MEMORY
	ANTERIOR	PREVIOUS
	PANTALLA	SCREEN
	TORMENTA	STORM
	SOLEADO	SUNNY
	DISCUTIR (ACALORADAMENTE)	TO ARGUE
	ASIGNAR	TO ASSIGN
	CONVOCAR UNA REUNION	TO CALL A MEETING
	EXIGIR	TO DEMAND
	ENFADARSE	TO GET ANGRY
	CARECER DE, FALTAR	TO LACK
	PROMOCIONAR, PROMOVER	TO PROMOTE
	DEPENDER DE (JERARQUICO)	TO REPORT TO
	SONREIR	TO SMILE
	PENSAR	TO THINK
	PESARSE	TO WEIGH
	JUNTOS	TOGETHER

	Spanish	English
	YA	ALREADY
	ATRACTIVO	ATTRACTIVE
	BENEFICIO	BENEFIT
	CUIDADOSO	CAREFUL
	CRUCIAL	CRUCIAL
	ENTORNO, MEDIO AMBIENTE	ENVIRONMENT
	GRACIOSO	FUNNY
	EN GENERAL	IN GENERAL
	MENSAJE	MESSAGE
	PRIORIDAD	PRIORITY
	RARAMENTE	SELDOM
	LA COMPETENCIA	THE COMPETITION
	LA LUNA	THE MOON
	AYUDAR	TO ASSIST
	FACTURAR	TO BILL
	SOPLAR	TO BLOW
	LLEVAR A CABO	TO CARRY OUT
	DESCRIBIR	TO DESCRIBE
	LLEGAR DE REGRESO	TO GET BACK
	REIRSE	TO LAUGH
	PROTEGER	TO PROTECT
	DESCANSAR	TO REST
	SELECCIONAR	TO SELECT
	RESOLVER	TO SOLVE
	TOCAR	TO TOUCH

	Spanish	English
	CANTIDAD, IMPORTE	AMOUNT
	ANTES DE	BEFORE
	HUESO	BONE
	CERCA DE	CLOSE TO
	PROFUNDO	DEEP
	EXPERTO	EXPERT
	ESPERANZA	HOPE
	PROBABLE	LIKELY
	VECINO	NEIGHBOR
	SOBRINO	NEPHEW
	PODER, POTENCIA	POWER
	SUELDO	SALARY
	EL COSTE	THE COST
	ESTAR DE BUEN HUMOR	TO BE IN A GOOD MOOD
	QUEJARSE DE	TO COMPLAIN ABOUT
	HACER HINCAPIE EN	TO EMPHASIZE
	BAJARSE DE	TO GET OFF
	SALIR	TO GO OUT
	CRECER	TO GROW
	PRESTAR ATENCION A	TO PAY ATTENTION TO
	RELAJARSE	TO RELAX
	SIMPLIFICAR	TO SIMPLIFY
	QUITARSE (ROPA)	TO TAKE OFF
	FEO	UGLY
	PESO	WEIGHT

	OTRA VEZ	AGAIN
	UNA OFERTA	AN OFFER
	DISPONIBLE	AVAILABLE
	BRASIL	BRAZIL
	OPORTUNIDAD, POSIBILIDAD	CHANCE
	CLIENTE	CUSTOMER
	TODO EL MUNDO	EVERYONE
	GENERALMENTE	GENERALLY
	A PESAR DE	IN SPITE OF
	ERROR	MISTAKE
	DE VEZ EN CUANDO	NOW AND THEN
	CARRERA	RACE
	SENCILLO	SIMPLE
	EXTRAÑO	STRANGE
	SUGERENCIA	SUGGESTION
	LLEGAR	TO ARRIVE
	QUEMAR, ARDER	TO BURN
	DEFENDER	TO DEFEND
	OLVIDAR	TO FORGET
	QUEDAR CON, GUARDAR	TO KEEP
	PROMETER	TO PROMISE
	EMPUJAR	TO PUSH
	ALQUILAR	TO RENT
	OLER	TO SMELL
	CUIDAR	TO TAKE CARE OF

ENFADADO	ANGRY
TIMBRE, CAMPANA	BELL
PORTAFOLIOS, CARTERA	BRIEFCASE
BRITANICO	BRITISH
ELECCION	CHOICE
FECHA TOPE, PLAZO	DEADLINE
TODO	EVERYTHING
AGRADECIDO	GRATEFUL
INCAPAZ DE	INCAPABLE OF
AGRADABLE	NICE
DE VERDAD	REALLY
ALGUN DIA	SOMEDAY
EL OTRO DIA ...	THE OTHER DAY ...
ESTAR DE MAL HUMOR	TO BE IN A BAD MOOD
CAMBIAR	TO CHANGE
COMPROBAR	TO CHECK
DEDICAR	TO DEVOTE
MEJORAR	TO GET BETTER
MARCHARSE	TO LEAVE
DEMOSTRAR	TO PROVE
DEJAR, ABANDONAR	TO QUIT
JUBILARSE	TO RETIRE
ESPECIFICAR	TO SPECIFY
APAGAR	TO TURN OFF
EQUIVOCADO	WRONG

	CUALQUIERA	ANYBODY
	CINTURON	BELT
	MOQUETA	CARPET
	COMPROMISO	COMMITMENT
	DECISION	DECISION
	EXCELENTE	EXCELLENT
	CORAZON	HEART
	CONOCIMIENTOS	KNOWLEDGE
	PUNTUAL	ON TIME
	PAQUETE	PACKAGE
	DOLOR	PAIN
	RAZONABLE	REASONABLE
	DISCURSO	SPEECH
	EL MUNDO	THE WORLD
	TENER SUERTE	TO BE LUCKY
	COMPARAR	TO COMPARE
	GANAR (TRABAJANDO)	TO EARN
	PREPARARSE PARA	TO GET READY FOR
	PRESTAR	TO LEND
	TIRAR (CONTRARIO DE EMPUJAR)	TO PULL
	REVISAR, REPASAR	TO REVIEW
	SEGUIR EN CONTACTO	TO STAY IN TOUCH
	ACTUALIZAR	TO UPDATE
	SEMAFORO	TRAFFIC LIGHT
	TIPICO	TYPICAL

	EN CUALQUIER SITIO	ANYPLACE
	FACTURA	BILL
	CALDERILLA, CAMBIO	CHANGE
	CIRCULO	CIRCLE
	CONFIANZA	CONFIDENCE
	SECO	DRY
	AMISTAD	FRIENDSHIP
	TIERRA	LAND
	PERSONAL (DE PLANTILLA)	PERSONNEL
	POSIBILIDAD	POSSIBILITY
	PROCESO	PROCESS
	TEJADO	ROOF
	ESTILO	STYLE
	NOMBRE	TO APPOINT
	CONSIDERAR	TO CONSIDER
	DISFRUTAR DE	TO ENJOY
	GARANTIZAR	TO GUARANTEE
	RECOGER	TO PICK UP
	QUITAR, EXTRAER	TO REMOVE
	ROBAR	TO STEAL
	APUNTAR	TO WRITE DOWN
	EL PARO	UNEMPLOYMENT
	VALOR	VALUE
	ENTERO	WHOLE
	PEOR	WORSE

	Spanish	English
	EN CUALQUIER SITIO	ANYWHERE
	ADEMAS DE	BESIDES
	LISTO, ASTUTO	CLEVER
	NUBE	CLOUD
	COMPAÑIA	COMPANY
	DETALLE	DETAIL
	GASTOS	EXPENSES
	ALTURA	HEIGHT
	IMAGINACION	IMAGINATION
	GERENTE, DIRECTOR	MANAGER
	PRESION	PRESSURE
	PROMESA	PROMISE
	TRANQUILAMENTE	QUIETLY
	SEGURIDAD (FISICA)	SAFETY
	DE EXITO, EXITOSO	SUCCESSFUL
	PERMITIR	TO ALLOW
	PEDIR PRESTADO	TO BORROW
	CRITICAR	TO CRITICIZE
	ESTIMAR	TO ESTIMATE
	MANTENER UNA REUNION	TO HOLD A MEETING
	MEDIR	TO MEASURE
	LLEGAR A UN ACUERDO	TO REACH AN AGREEMENT
	AHORRAR	TO SAVE
	SUGERIR	TO SUGGEST
	DIA DE LA SEMANA LABORAL	WEEKDAY

	POR LO VISTO, AL PARECER	APPARENTLY
	JEFE	BOSS
	PASE	COME IN
	COMPETENTE	COMPETENT
	DUDA	DOUBT
	EXPLICACION	EXPLANATION
	AGUJERO	HOLE
	VAGO, PEREZOSO	LAZY
	PINTURA	PAINTING
	RECIENTE	RECENT
	RESPETO	RESPECT
	SERIO	SERIOUS
	ETAPA	STAGE
	EL PEOR	THE WORST
	SUPONER, ASUMIR	TO ASSUME
	SER PESIMISTA	TO BE PESSIMISTIC
	TRAER	TO BRING
	CRUZAR	TO CROSS
	FRACASAR	TO FAIL
	INVITAR	TO INVITE
	OFENDER	TO OFFEND
	PRESIONAR	TO PRESSURE
	REFERIRSE A	TO REFER TO
	VENDER	TO SELL
	SORPRENDER	TO SURPRISE

	ASPECTO	ASPECT
	NEGOCIO	BUSINESS
	COSTUMBRE	CUSTOM
	PELIGRO	DANGER
	DIBUJO	DRAWING
	FLEXIBLE	FLEXIBLE
	VIDA	LIFE
	POBLACION	POPULATION
	DESDE QUE, PUESTO QUE	SINCE
	PIEL	SKIN
	HISTORIA, CUENTO	STORY
	ESTAR DE ACUERDO	TO AGREE
	PONERSE EN CONTACTO CON	TO CONTACT
	ESTABLECER	TO ESTABLISH
	DEJAR, PERMITIR	TO LET
	ALCANZAR	TO REACH
	SERVIR	TO SERVE
	DESPERDICIAR, MALGASTAR	TO WASTE
	TOTALMENTE	TOTALLY
	TRATAMIENTO	TREATMENT
	INESPERADO	UNEXPECTED
	HASTA	UNTIL
	DEBIL	WEAK
	¿ QUE PASA ?	WHAT'S THE MATTER ?
	MADERA	WOOD

AL PRINCIPIO	AT FIRST
CONFIRMACION	CONFIRMATION
DEFINICION	DEFINITION
GRADO	DEGREE
GRAN ALMACEN	DEPARTMENT STORE
DURANTE	DURING
ME ALEGRO	I'M GLAD
PERDIDA	LOSS
RIESGO	RISK
FUERZA	STRENGTH
TONTO	STUPID
LA ENSEÑANZA	TEACHING
COMENZAR	TO BEGIN
COPIAR	TO COPY
CONSEGUIR RESULTADOS	TO GET RESULTS
MANTENER	TO MAINTAIN
ESTROPEAR	TO RUIN
TENER EXITO, TRIUNFAR	TO SUCCEED
DURO, DIFICIL	TOUGH
PROBLEMAS	TROUBLE
DESAFORTUNADAMENTE	UNFORTUNATELY
INUTIL	USELESS
¿ QUE QUIERES DECIR ?	WHAT DO YOU MEAN ?
DENTRO DE	WITHIN
PREOCUPADO	WORRIED

FONDO, PARTE INFERIOR	BOTTOM
CURSO	COURSE
DESIERTO	DESERT
SUEÑO	DREAM
FAMOSO	FAMOUS
CAMPO	FIELD
HIELO	ICE
AGRADABLE	PLEASANT
SEGURO (LIBRE DE PELIGRO)	SAFE
LA PARTE FRONTAL	THE FRONT
LAS NOTICIAS	THE NEWS
DELGADO	THIN
BENEFICIARSE DE	TO BENEFIT FROM
ELIMINAR	TO ELIMINATE
DEVOLVER	TO GIVE BACK
PONERSE (ROPA)	TO PUT ON
SATISFACER	TO SATISFY
APROVECHAR	TO TAKE ADVANTAGE OF
ATASCO DE TRAFICO	TRAFFIC JAM
VERDADERO, VERDAD	TRUE
IMPROBABLE	UNLIKELY
VISTA	VIEW
¿ QUE CLASE DE ...?	WHAT KIND OF ...?
MARAVILLOSO	WONDERFUL
PEOR QUE	WORSE THAN

	ASCENSOR	ELEVATOR
	ENTRADA	ENTRANCE
	EQUIPAMIENTO	EQUIPMENT
	HACIA ADELANTE	FORWARD
	FRECUENTEMENTE	FREQUENTLY
	ORO	GOLD
	LA GRAMATICA	GRAMMAR
	GRAN BRETAÑA	GREAT BRITAIN
	ARMA DE FUEGO	GUN
	GUAPO, APUESTO	HANDSOME
	APENAS	HARDLY
	IDENTICO	IDENTICAL
	IRLANDA	IRELAND
	CHISTE	JOKE
	GRANDE	LARGE
	LECHUGA	LETTUCE
	BAJO	LOW
	LA COSTA	THE COAST
	HACER PUBLICIDAD	TO ADVERTISE
	AYUDAR	TO AID
	MORDER	TO BITE
	COMPLETAR	TO COMPLETE
	GANAR, ADQUIRIR	TO GAIN
	CASARSE	TO GET MARRIED
	INSISTIR EN	TO INSIST ON

	INGENIERO	ENGINEER
	VUELO	FLIGHT
	CONGELADO	FROZEN
	SIGNIFICADO	MEANING
	SUEGRA	MOTHER-IN-LAW
	MEDIODIA	NOON
	DE VEZ EN CUANDO	OCCASIONALLY
	PROPIO	OWN
	PASAJERO	PASSENGER
	PASTILLA, PILDORA	PILL
	POSIBLEMENTE	POSSIBLY
	PRODUCTO	PRODUCT
	PARIENTES	RELATIVES
	DUCHA	SHOWER
	SILENCIOSO	SILENT
	EN ALGUNA PARTE	SOMEWHERE
	ORTOGRAFIA	SPELLING
	DIENTES	TEETH
	EXAMEN, ENSAYO	TEST
	OBTENER	TO OBTAIN
	SUFRIR	TO SUFFER
	TURISMO	TOURISM
	TIPICAMENTE	TYPICALLY
	GUERRA	WAR
	SIN	WITHOUT

Vocabulary booklet 3
NIVEL INTERMEDIO

LIST I

	UNA CALLE DE DOBLE SENTIDO	A TWO-WAY STREET
	ANUNCIO (EN PRENSA)	AD
	ADVERSARIO	ADVERSARY
	BICHO	BUG
	ESCUETO, CONCISO	CONCISE
	INGENIERIA	ENGINEERING
	PROHIBIDO	FORBIDDEN
	CALOR	HEAT
	ESCONDIDO, OCULTO	HIDDEN
	IMPARCIAL	IMPARTIAL
	IMPACIENTE	IMPATIENT
	CLASE MEDIA	MIDDLE CLASS
	MISTERIOSO	MYSTERIOUS
	PESIMISTA	PESSIMISTIC
	IMPORTANTE, SIGNIFICATIVO	SIGNIFICANT
	SINCERIDAD	SINCERITY
	ESTRATEGICO	STRATEGIC
	AFECTAR	TO AFFECT
	DICTAR	TO DICTATE
	PROHIBIR	TO FORBID
	IMPRESIONAR	TO IMPRESS
	COSER	TO SEW
	AGRADECER	TO THANK
	DAR LA BIENVENIDA	TO WELCOME
	RARO	UNCOMMON

LIST 2

	ABUNDANTE	ABUNDANT
	CARIÑOSO	AFFECTIONATE
	ASI COMO	AS WELL AS
	DURMIENDO, DORMIDO	ASLEEP
	JAULA	CAGE
	CALEFACCION CENTRAL	CENTRAL HEATING
	FRESCO (TEMPERATURA)	COOL
	FANATICO	FANATIC
	BASURA	GARBAGE
	MIEL	HONEY
	POR ADELANTADO	IN ADVANCE
	MIENTRAS TANTO	IN THE MEANTIME
	LONGITUD	LENGTH
	MEDIANOCHE	MIDNIGHT
	NATIVO	NATIVE
	PSICOLOGICO	PSYCHOLOGICAL
	FRESAS	STRAWBERRIES
	AGRADECIDO	THANKFUL
	LOGRAR, LLEVAR A CABO	TO ACCOMPLISH
	DESAPARECER	TO DISAPPEAR
	FLUIR	TO FLOW
	OBLIGAR	TO FORCE
	REPARAR	TO REPAIR
	HUNDIR	TO SINK
	DEBAJO DE	UNDERNEATH

LIST 3

	ADECUADAMENTE	ADEQUATELY
	AGRESIVO	AGGRESSIVE
	NACIMIENTO	BIRTH
	MANTA	BLANKET
	PRESUPUESTO	BUDGET
	ELEGANTE	ELEGANT
	TEMOR, MIEDO	FEAR
	FRUSTRANTE	FRUSTRATING
	LUNA DE MIEL	HONEYMOON
	EN TEORIA	IN THEORY
	NATURALMENTE	NATURALLY
	PREDOMINANTE	PREDOMINANT
	TRIMESTRALMENTE	QUARTERLY
	MAQUINA DE COSER	SEWING MACHINE
	ESTRICTO	STRICT
	ASEGURAR	TO ASSURE
	COBRAR, CARGAR	TO CHARGE
	CONTENER	TO CONTAIN
	DESCUBRIR	TO DISCOVER
	PREVER	TO FORECAST
	MANTENER UNA REUNION	TO HOLD A MEETING
	SALTAR, OMITIR	TO SKIP
	SEGUIR EN CONTACTO	TO STAY IN TOUCH
	ROPA INTERIOR	UNDERWEAR
	BIENESTAR	WELL-BEING

LIST 4

VENTAJOSO	ADVANTAGEOUS
FOLLETO	BROCHURE
¡ ENHORABUENA !	CONGRATULATIONS !
CONSIDERABLE	CONSIDERABLE
SALIDA	DEPARTURE
LIBERTAD	FREEDOM
AJO	GARLIC
OFICINA CENTRAL	HEADQUARTERS
IMPLANTACION	IMPLEMENTATION
IMPRESCINDIBLE	INDISPENSABLE
NECESIDAD	NECESSITY
PREDECIBLE	PREDICTABLE
PROMINENTE	PROMINENT
SENTIDO	SENSE
ESCLAVO	SLAVE
AUNQUE	THOUGH
MERECER	TO DESERVE
EXTENDER, PRORROGAR	TO EXTEND
CUMPLIR	TO FULFILL
DECLARARSE EN HUELGA	TO GO ON STRIKE
CAZAR	TO HUNT
HACER DAÑO, DOLER	TO HURT
INDICAR	TO INDICATE
EN PARO	UNEMPLOYED
FAMOSO, CONOCIDO	WELL-KNOWN

LIST 5

UNA PERDIDA DE TIEMPO	A WASTE OF TIME
AYUDA, AUXILIO	AID
COMPORTAMIENTO	BEHAVIOR
MANDON	BOSSY
COMPARABLE	COMPARABLE
HECHO	FACT
FORMATO	FORMAT
RAYO, RELAMPAGO	LIGHTNING
NERVIOS	NERVES
DOLOROSO	PAINFUL
SOMBRA	SHADE
DORMIDO, CON SUEÑO	SLEEPY
AMENAZA	THREAT
LOGRAR, CONSEGUIR	TO ACHIEVE
ESTAR EN HUELGA	TO BE ON STRIKE
ECHAR LA CULPA A	TO BLAME
FORMAR ACADEMICAMENTE	TO EDUCATE
LUCHAR, PELEAR	TO FIGHT
FLOTAR	TO FLOAT
DOBLAR, PLEGAR	TO FOLD
ENGORDAR	TO GAIN WEIGHT
GUIAR	TO GUIDE
IMPLANTAR, PONER EN MARCHA	TO IMPLEMENT
DESAFORTUNADAMENTE	UNFORTUNATELY
BALLENA	WHALE

UNA GRABACION	A RECORDING
AGIL	AGILE
EMBAJADOR	AMBASSADOR
DESCUIDADO	CARELESS
NUBLADO	CLOUDY
EFICIENTE	EFFICIENT
CARA A CARA	FACE-TO-FACE
PLENA JORNADA	FULL TIME
IDEAL	IDEAL
INCIDENTE	INCIDENT
INDICE	INDEX
EN PRINCIPIO	INITIALLY
INTENSO	INTENSE
MANO DE OBRA	LABOR
COMIDA	MEAL
NORUEGA	NORWAY
A PIE / ANDANDO	ON FOOT
PRECEDENTE, ANTERIOR	PRECEDING
¿Y QUE ?	SO WHAT ?
A LO LARGO Y ANCHO DE	THROUGHOUT
RESERVAR	TO BOOK
TEMER	TO FEAR
INFLUIR EN	TO INFLUENCE
UNICO EN SU GENERO	UNIQUE
TRIGO	WHEAT

LIST 7

1	PRECISO, EXACTO	ACCURATE
2	DECISIVO	DECISIVE
3	DESTINO	DESTINATION
4	EMBAJADA	EMBASSY
5	VENTILADOR, ABANICO	FAN
6	OLVIDADIZO	FORGETFUL
7	FRAGIL	FRAGILE
8	DOLOR DE CABEZA	HEADACHE
9	IDENTIDAD	IDENTITY
10	INCOMPETENCIA	INCOMPETENCE
11	INICIATIVA	INITIATIVE
12	MENTIROSO	LIAR
13	ASUNTO	MATTER
14	ALCALDE	MAYOR
15	NORUEGO	NORWEGIAN
16	LIGERAMENTE	SLIGHTLY
17	MALETA	SUITCASE
18	TRUENO	THUNDER
19	APOSTAR	TO BET
20	DAR DE COMER, ALIMENTAR	TO FEED
21	CABER	TO FIT
22	MENTIR	TO LIE
23	AGITAR, TEMBLAR	TO SHAKE
24	UNIR	TO UNITE
25	SI	WHETHER

	MUCHO	A GREAT DEAL OF
	ANTEPASADO	ANCESTOR
	BILINGUE	BILINGUAL
	CUEVA	CAVE
	PROFUNDAMENTE	DEEPLY
	MARCO (DE UN CUADRO)	FRAME
	SIMPATICO, AMIGABLE	FRIENDLY
	IDIOTA	IDIOT
	TINTA	INK
	HORAS EXTRAS	OVERTIME
	PARCIALMENTE	PARTIALLY
	PREFERIBLE	PREFERABLE
	PREMATURO	PREMATURE
	PRESTIGIOSO	PRESTIGIOUS
	PRETEXTO	PRETEXT
	RESISTENTE	RESISTANT
	RIDICULO	RIDICULOUS
	SERIE	SERIES
	ESBELTO	SLIM
	SUMA	SUM
	LA TIERRA	THE EARTH
	PENSAR HACER, PROGRAMAR	TO PLAN
	ATAR	TO TIE
	DESCONOCIDO	UNKNOWN
	VIUDA	WIDOW

LIST 9

	UN ATAJO	A SHORTCUT
	DISCIPLINA	DISCIPLINE
	PARA SIEMPRE	FOREVER
	PASTOR ALEMAN	GERMAN SHEPHERD
	CHISMORREO	GOSSIP
	AURICULARES	HEADPHONES
	LIDER	LEADER
	CERCANO	NEARBY
	SIMPLE, SIN AIRES	PLAIN
	PRAGMATICO	PRAGMATIC
	ARRIESGADO	RISKY
	ESCANDALO	SCANDAL
	LISTO, ELEGANTE	SMART
	RESUMEN	SUMMARY
	APRETADO	TIGHT
	EXPORTAR	TO EXPORT
	ODIAR	TO HATE
	DUDAR, VACILAR	TO HESITATE
	INSPECCIONAR	TO INSPECT
	LEVANTAR	TO LIFT
	ECHAR DE MENOS, PERDER	TO MISS
	RECORDAR	TO RECALL
	DAR LA MANO	TO SHAKE HANDS
	A NO SER QUE	UNLESS
	ANCHURA	WIDTH

	Spanish	English
	CADA UNO	APIECE
	A VECES	AT TIMES
	NIÑEZ	CHILDHOOD
	CREATIVO	CREATIVE
	DERROTA	DEFEAT
	DESACUERDO	DISAGREEMENT
	EMPLEADO	EMPLOYEE
	BOSQUE	FOREST
	EN CONTACTO CON	IN CONTACT WITH
	EN REALIDAD	IN REALITY
	INTROVERTIDO	INTROVERTED
	MAQUILLAJE	MAKEUP
	FILOSOFICO	PHILOSOPHICAL
	POTENCIAL	POTENTIAL
	PRACTICAMENTE	PRACTICALLY
	AHORROS	SAVINGS
	POCO PROFUNDO, SOMERO	SHALLOW
	OLOR	SMELL
	SUPERFICIAL	SUPERFICIAL
	ENCENDER (CIGARRO, FUEGO)	TO LIGHT
	RELACIONAR EN UNA LISTA	TO LIST
	LLEGAR A DOMINAR	TO MASTER
	HACER LAS MALETAS	TO PACK
	DESCARGAR	TO UNLOAD
	SALVAJE	WILD

LIST 11

	IRA, RABIA, ENFADO	ANGER
	QUE YO SEPA	AS FAR AS I KNOW
	EN CUALQUIER CASO	AT ANY RATE
	AMARGO	BITTER
	AVERIA, DESGLOSE	BREAKDOWN
	BREVEMENTE	BRIEFLY
	EMOCIONANTE	EXCITING
	FORTUNA	FORTUNE
	FUNCIONAL	FUNCTIONAL
	GITANO	GYPSY
	INMEDIATO	IMMEDIATE
	EQUIPAJE	LUGGAGE
	EVIDENTE, OBVIO	OBVIOUS
	POBREZA	POVERTY
	PRACTICA	PRACTICE
	BILLETE DE VUELTA	RETURN TICKET
	SONRISA	SMILE
	SUMINISTRO	SUPPLY
	SOLICITAR	TO APPLY FOR
	ESPERAR, PREVER	TO EXPECT
	INVENTAR	TO INVENT
	CARGAR	TO LOAD
	CUIDAR (DE ALGUIEN)	TO LOOK AFTER
	PARTICIPAR	TO PARTICIPATE
	PERIODO DE PRUEBA	TRIAL PERIOD

	ATRACTIVO	APPEAL
	MARCA	BRAND
	PREOCUPADO	CONCERNED
	DAÑADO	DAMAGED
	ECONOMICO	ECONOMIC
	ENVIDIOSO	ENVIOUS
	EMOCIONADO	EXCITED
	EXTRANJERO (ADJETIVO)	FOREIGN
	ANFITRION	HOST
	CAZADOR	HUNTER
	INMIGRANTE	IMMIGRANT
	INVENTO	INVENTION
	MAQUINARIA	MACHINERY
	PRINCIPALMENTE	MAINLY
	MANTENIMIENTO	MAINTENANCE
	MEZCLA	MIXTURE
	POR TELEFONO	ON THE PHONE
	PACIENTE	PATIENT
	PRODUCTIVIDAD	PRODUCTIVITY
	PROFESIONALIDAD	PROFESSIONALISM
	FORMA, CONFIGURACION	SHAPE
	DISCUTIR (ACALORADAMENTE)	TO ARGUE
	ESTIMAR	TO ESTIMATE
	SALUDAR	TO GREET
	DEBER	TO OWE

LIST 13

	VALLA PUBLICITARIA	BILLBOARD
	CAMPAÑA	CAMPAIGN
	CAJERO	CASHIER
	EXCUSA	EXCUSE
	AUTENTICO	GENUINE
	IMPACTO	IMPACT
	INCOMPETENTE	INCOMPETENT
	MINIMO	MINIMUM
	PERMANENTEMENTE	PERMANENTLY
	PERTINENTE, CORRESPONDIENTE	PERTINENT
	APLAZAMIENTO	POSTPONEMENT
	PARA QUE ...	SO THAT ...
	APOYO, RESPALDO	SUPPORT
	APLICAR	TO APPLY
	COBRAR	TO COLLECT
	ADJUNTAR (A UNA CARTA)	TO ENCLOSE
	EXAMINAR	TO EXAMINE
	ADIVINAR, SUPONER	TO GUESS
	INFORMAR	TO INFORM
	INVESTIGAR	TO INVESTIGATE
	PROGRESAR	TO PROGRESS
	COMPARTIR	TO SHARE
	DEJAR PROPINA	TO TIP
	DESAGRADABLE	UNPLEASANT
	FUERZA DE VOLUNTAD	WILLPOWER

	ETCETERA	AND SO ON
	TASA DE NATALIDAD	BIRTH RATE
	DEPRIMIDO	DEPRESSED
	NIEBLA	FOG
	PLENAMENTE	FULLY
	FANTASMA	GHOST
	SUPERMERCADO	GROCERY STORE
	INVITACION	INVITATION
	POR SI ACASO	JUST IN CASE
	FLOJO, SUELTO	LOOSE
	MADURO	MATURE
	PERMISO	PERMISSION
	LA POLITICA	POLITICS
	PROCEDIMIENTO	PROCEDURE
	ACCIONISTA	SHAREHOLDER
	HUELGA	STRIKE
	HACER EJERCICIO	TO EXERCISE
	TENER INTENCION DE	TO INTEND
	INCORPORARSE A, UNIRSE A	TO JOIN
	DEJAR UNA PROPINA	TO LEAVE A TIP
	PROHIBIR, IMPEDIR	TO PROHIBIT
	PROPONER	TO PROPOSE
	APOYAR, MANTENER	TO SUPPORT
	IMPOPULAR	UNPOPULAR
	VENTOSO	WINDY

1	COMO SI	AS THOUGH
2	PRIMA, INCENTIVO	BONUS
3	DIBUJOS ANIMADOS	CARTOONS
4	DESDE LUEGO, POR SUPUESTO	CERTAINLY
5	CONSERVADOR	CONSERVATIVE
6	DISEÑO	DESIGN
7	SALIDA	EXIT
8	UÑA	FINGERNAIL
9	MOSCA	FLY
10	PERIODISTA	JOURNALIST
11	REINO	KINGDOM
12	LOGICAMENTE	LOGICALLY
13	NINGUNA PARTE	NOWHERE
14	FUERA DE CONTROL	OUT OF CONTROL
15	PORTATIL	PORTABLE
16	PRECAUCION	PRECAUTION
17	CUALIFICADO	QUALIFIED
18	NEUMATICO	TIRE
19	INVOLUCRAR	TO INVOLVE
20	BAJAR, HACER DESCENDER	TO LOWER
21	POSPONER	TO POSTPONE
22	PROCEDER	TO PROCEED
23	SUPONER	TO SUPPOSE
24	RARO	UNUSUAL
25	ALA	WING

	GANGA, CHOLLO	BARGAIN
	ENVIDIA	ENVY
	CON SOLTURA	FLUENTLY
	PEGAMENTO	GLUE
	A MITAD DE CAMINO	HALFWAY
	INFARTO	HEART ATTACK
	MAL EDUCADO	IMPOLITE
	EN CONTEXTO	IN CONTEXT
	JUGO, ZUMO	JUICE
	INFERIOR, MAS BAJO	LOWER
	MILAGRO	MIRACLE
	PERSUASIVO	PERSUASIVE
	FILOSOFIA	PHILOSOPHY
	PRECISO, EXACTO	PRECISE
	LA PRENSA	THE PRESS
	EXPLORAR	TO EXPLORE
	VESTIRSE	TO GET DRESSED
	REUNIRSE	TO GET TOGETHER
	IMPORTAR	TO IMPORT
	BROMEAR	TO JOKE
	JUZGAR	TO JUDGE
	FINGIR	TO PRETEND
	BENEFICIARSE DE	TO PROFIT FROM
	INACEPTABLE	UNACCEPTABLE
	GANADOR	WINNER

	HERMOSURA, BELLEZA	BEAUTY
	CIUDADANO	CITIZEN
	CAJON	DRAWER
	EXPORTACIONES	EXPORTS
	SOLTURA	FLUENCY
	ULTRAMARINOS, COMESTIBLES	GROCERIES
	PEINADO	HAIRSTYLE
	AUDICION, CAPACIDAD AUDITIVA	HEARING
	POCO A POCO	LITTLE BY LITTLE
	SUERTE, FORTUNA	LUCK
	ESPEJO	MIRROR
	BARRIO	NEIGHBORHOOD
	PARRAFO	PARAGRAPH
	PRECISAMENTE	PRECISELY
	RECESION	RECESSION
	EGOISTA	SELFISH
	SOLDADO	SOLDIER
	LA LEY	THE LAW
	PREDECIR	TO PREDICT
	PULSAR	TO PRESS
	PREVENIR, EVITAR	TO PREVENT
	SOBREVIVIR	TO SURVIVE
	HERRAMIENTA	TOOL
	VARIEDAD	VARIETY
	ALAMBRE, CABLE	WIRE

	MAS ALLA DE	BEYOND
	CEREBRO	BRAIN
	DISCUSION (NO ACALORADA)	DISCUSSION
	DE MODA	IN FASHION
	INVISIBLE	INVISIBLE
	MEDIDAS	MEASUREMENTS
	MALENTENDIDO	MISUNDERSTANDING
	¡ DIOS MIO !	MY GOD !
	ENCIMA DE	ON TOP OF
	MONTON	PILE
	CONTENTO	PLEASED
	SACERDOTE, CURA	PRIEST
	PERFIL	PROFILE
	PERSPECTIVAS	PROSPECTS
	REFERENCIA	REFERENCE
	MARISCOS	SHELLFISH
	LEVE, LIGERO	SLIGHT
	SOLIDO	SOLID
	SUPERVIVIENTE	SURVIVOR
	EL COSTE DE LA VIDA	THE COST OF LIVING
	PERMITIRSE EL LUJO DE	TO AFFORD
	EXPRESAR	TO EXPRESS
	CONCEDER	TO GRANT
	VARIAR	TO VARY
	INTELIGENTE, SABIO	WISE

LIST 19

	UN REQUISITO	A REQUIREMENT
	FRENOS	BRAKES
	POR CASUALIDAD	BY CHANCE
	PAPEL CARTON	CARDBOARD
	CONSECUTIVO, SEGUIDO	CONSECUTIVE
	DEUDA	DEBT
	DESCUENTO	DISCOUNT
	EXPRESIVO	EXPRESSIVE
	PLANO, LLANO	FLAT
	PARA SIEMPRE	FOR GOOD
	TRABAJADOR	HARD-WORKING
	JOYA	JEWEL
	LEGAL	LEGAL
	PARA NADA, EN ABSOLUTO	NOT AT ALL
	DE SOBRA	PLENTY OF
	PRIVADO, INTIMO	PRIVATE
	CORRECTAMENTE, ADECUADAMENTE	PROPERLY
	PROSPERIDAD	PROSPERITY
	MATERIA, COSA, SUSTANCIA	STUFF
	HACER UN ESFUERZO	TO MAKE AN EFFORT
	SEÑALAR, RESALTAR	TO POINT OUT
	TRAGAR	TO SWALLOW
	DESEAR	TO WISH
	TEMA (DE CONVERSACION)	TOPIC
	VEHICULO	VEHICLE

	Spanish	English
	ALOJAMIENTO	ACCOMMODATIONS
	CAMPAÑA PUBLICITARIA	ADVERTISING CAMPAIGN
	SUCURSAL, RAMA	BRANCH
	VALIENTE	BRAVE
	CANCELACION	CANCELLATION
	DECENTE	DECENT
	EXTRAORDINARIO	EXTRAORDINARY
	FABULOSO	FABULOUS
	FALSA ALARMA	FALSE ALARM
	PRECIOSO	GORGEOUS
	UTIL	HANDY
	IMPERSONAL	IMPERSONAL
	JUDIO	JEW
	LIMITE	LIMIT
	NI .... NI	NEITHER .... NOR
	PAZ	PEACE
	PECULIAR	PECULIAR
	POLITICO	POLITICIAN
	PREDICCION	PREDICTION
	RENTABILIDAD	PROFITABILITY
	PROVISIONAL, TEMPORAL	PROVISIONAL
	REALISTA	REALISTIC
	SEÑALAR	TO POINT
	PREGUNTARSE	TO WONDER
	VICE VERSA	VICE VERSA

	Spanish	English
	ACEPTACION	ACCEPTANCE
	CONTABLE	ACCOUNTANT
	EXTROVERTIDO	EXTROVERTED
	BANDERA	FLAG
	FRACCION	FRACTION
	PATATAS FRITAS	FRENCH FRIES
	INFLEXIBLE	INFLEXIBLE
	INESTABILIDAD	INSTABILITY
	RENTABLE	PROFITABLE
	LECTURA	READING
	RECIBO	RECEIPT
	ENVIO (DE MERCANCIAS)	SHIPMENT
	FUENTE, ORIGEN	SOURCE
	SORPRENDENTE	SURPRISING
	INTERRUPTOR	SWITCH
	LAS RAMAS	THE BRANCHES
	LA DIRECCION	THE MANAGEMENT
	GOBERNAR	TO GOVERN
	ECHAR AL CORREO	TO MAIL
	PROPORCIONAR, SUMINISTRAR	TO PROVIDE
	PROVOCAR	TO PROVOKE
	COMERCIO	TRADE
	DESAFORTUNADO	UNLUCKY
	VICTIMA	VICTIM
	TALLER MECANICO	WORKSHOP

CATEGORIA	CATEGORY
COMPETITIVO	COMPETITIVE
CONSIDERADO	CONSIDERATE
ABARROTADO	CROWDED
ECONOMISTA	ECONOMIST
ARCHIVADOR	FILING CABINET
SABOR	FLAVOR
INCENDIO FORESTAL	FOREST FIRE
LUNA LLENA	FULL MOON
GOBERNADOR	GOVERNOR
EN VISTA DE	IN VIEW OF
INDIFERENTE	INDIFFERENT
ZURDO	LEFT-HANDED
PARANOICO	PARANOID
PRESTIGIO	PRESTIGE
DEMOSTRACION, PRUEBA	PROOF
DUDOSO	QUESTIONABLE
PESCADO Y MARISCO	SEAFOOD
ESPECIALISTA	SPECIALIST
VALER LA PENA	TO BE WORTH IT
REALIZAR	TO PERFORM
PUBLICAR	TO PUBLISH
CAMBIAR	TO SWITCH
TRADUCIR	TO TRANSLATE
DISPUESTO	WILLING

	LOGRO, CONSECUCION	ACCOMPLISHMENT
	ACONSEJABLE	ADVISABLE
	APETITO	APPETITE
	BALA	BULLET
	CONFIDENCIAL	CONFIDENTIAL
	ACTUAL	CURRENT
	REGLA DE ORO	GOLDEN RULE
	INDEFINIDAMENTE	INDEFINITELY
	ALTAVOZ	LOUDSPEAKER
	PARADOJICO	PARADOXICAL
	FONTANERO	PLUMBER
	ANTERIORMENTE	PREVIOUSLY
	ADECUADO	PROPER
	BASTANTE	QUITE
	BUSQUEDA	SEARCH
	LISO	SMOOTH
	PROPINA	TIP
	VALER LA PENA	TO BE WORTHWHILE
	ATERRIZAR, TOMAR TIERRA	TO LAND
	MEMORIZAR	TO MEMORIZE
	CUESTIONAR	TO QUESTION
	ESPECIALIZARSE	TO SPECIALIZE
	ENCENDER	TO SWITCH ON
	BANDEJA	TRAY
	VOLUMEN	VOLUME

	CONSCIENTE DE	AWARE OF
	CIEGO	BLIND
	SANGRE	BLOOD
	AVERGONZADO, VIOLENTO	EMBARRASSED
	EL OTOÑO	FALL
	DIRECTRICES	GUIDELINES
	ENCABEZAMIENTO	HEADING
	NIÑOS, HIJOS	KIDS
	PREFERIBLEMENTE	PREFERABLY
	PROMETEDOR	PROMISING
	CUOTA	QUOTA
	REACCION	REACTION
	ESPECIFICAMENTE	SPECIFICALLY
	EL CANAL DE LA MANCHA	THE ENGLISH CHANNEL
	GRADUARSE	TO GRADUATE
	CERRAR CON LLAVE	TO LOCK
	MENCIONAR	TO MENTION
	IMPRIMIR	TO PRINT
	BUSCAR	TO SEARCH FOR
	PROPORCIONAR, SUMINISTRAR	TO SUPPLY
	APAGAR	TO SWITCH OFF
	TRIPLICAR	TO TRIPLE
	ENVOLVER	TO WRAP
	TESORO	TREASURE
	CINTURA	WAIST

	A TODA VELOCIDAD	AT FULL SPEED
	AUTENTICO	AUTHENTIC
	BASADO EN	BASED ON
	CAPITULO	CHAPTER
	CHICLE	CHEWING GUM
	HARINA	FLOUR
	GRATITUD	GRATITUDE
	GRIEGO	GREEK
	¡ ESPERA !	HOLD ON !
	ANFITRIONA	HOSTESS
	POR ESCRITO	IN WRITING
	INVERSION	INVESTMENT
	PRESTAMO	LOAN
	MINA	MINE
	EMBARAZADA	PREGNANT
	ASCENSO, PROMOCION	PROMOTION
	EMISORA DE RADIO	RADIO STATION
	CIENCIA	SCIENCE
	VELOCIDAD	SPEED
	SISTEMATICO	SYSTEMATIC
	DIMINUTO, MUY PEQUEÑO	TINY
	ESTAR FAMILIARIZADO CON	TO BE FAMILIAR WITH
	DISPARA	TO SHOOT
	TRATAR	TO TREAT
	CARTERA, BILLETERO	WALLET

	UNA PETICION	A REQUEST
	PUENTE	BRIDGE
	CARACTER	CHARACTER
	ELOCUENTE	ELOQUENT
	TARIFA	FARE
	LA FRENTE	FOREHEAD
	GRECIA	GREECE
	GARANTIA	GUARANTEE
	SEMANA SANTA	HOLY WEEK
	IMPULSIVO	IMPULSIVE
	EN COMUN	IN COMMON
	MINORIA	MINORITY
	ORGANIZADO	ORGANIZED
	PUERTO (DE MAR)	PORT
	INMEDIATO, RAPIDO, PRONTO	PROMPT
	FERROCARRIL	RAILROAD
	ESPIRITU	SPIRIT
	TALENTO	TALENT
	LO SIGUIENTE	THE FOLLOWING
	DUPLICAR	TO DOUBLE
	SUBIR, ELEVAR	TO RAISE
	ADVERTIR	TO WARN
	TENDENCIA	TREND
	INNECESARIO	UNNECESSARY
	ESCRITO	WRITTEN

	CONTABILIDAD	ACCOUNTING
	DINERO EN METALICO	CASH
	CONEXION	CONNECTION
	PRESA	DAM
	DECADA	DECADE
	POLVO	DUST
	EFICIENCIA	EFFICIENCY
	AGRICULTURA	FARMING
	FAVORABLE	FAVORABLE
	GUARDA	GUARD
	TRABAJO DOMESTICO	HOUSEWORK
	LESION	INJURY
	VESTIBULO (DE HOTEL)	LOBBY
	MODESTO	MODEST
	LLUVIOSO	RAINY
	GAMA	RANGE
	VALORACION	RATING
	ORILLA	SHORE
	DEPOSITO	TANK
	EL CONTENIDO	THE CONTENTS
	ESTAR DISPUESTO A	TO BE WILLING TO
	DIVIDIR	TO SPLIT
	TRUCO, TRAMPA	TRICK
	ADVERTENCIA	WARNING
	ANUALMENTE	YEARLY

VIVO	ALIVE
TABLON DE ANUNCIOS	BULLETIN BOARD
COMPLICADO	COMPLICATED
CONCESIONARIO	DEALER
LA MUERTE	DEATH
BORRACHO, BEBIDO	DRUNK
UN DIA SI Y OTRO NO	EVERY OTHER DAY
CULPA	FAULT
PREVISION	FORECAST
PUNTO FINAL	FULL STOP
FONDOS	FUNDS
INVITADO, HUESPED	GUEST
IMPRESION	IMPRESSION
INCOMPATIBLE	INCOMPATIBLE
PENDIENTE	PENDING
SALADO	SALTY
SERIAMENTE	SERIOUSLY
A CORTO PLAZO	SHORT-TERM
ESPONTANEO	SPONTANEOUS
PASO A PASO	STEP BY STEP
BLANCO, OBJETIVO	TARGET
ESTAR METIDO EN UN LIO	TO BE IN TROUBLE
MODIFICAR	TO MODIFY
PAPELERA	WASTE BASKET
JUVENTUD	YOUTH

LIST 29

	ASOMBROSO	AMAZING
	CORRIDA DE TOROS	BULLFIGHT
	PRESIDENTE DEL CONSEJO	CHAIRMAN
	COMPATIBLE	COMPATIBLE
	CONTAGIOSO	CONTAGIOUS
	TRIBUNAL	COURT
	POSTRE	DESSERT
	HEMBRA	FEMALE
	GUIA	GUIDE
	IMPROBABLE	IMPROBABLE
	LABIOS	LIPS
	UBICADO	LOCATED
	MATRIMONIO	MARRIAGE
	OPERACION	OPERATION
	PLACER	PLEASURE
	RESPONSABLE	RESPONSIBLE
	SEGURO	SECURE
	ESPONTANEAMENTE	SPONTANEOUSLY
	TAREA	TASK
	A TRAVES DE	THROUGH
	LLEVARSE BIEN CON	TO GET ALONG WITH
	RAZONAR CON	TO REASON WITH
	CONFIANZA	TRUST
	OLA	WAVE
	¡ QUE LIO !	WHAT A MESS !

UNA CALLE DE SENTIDO UNICO	A ONE-WAY STREET
LA HISTORIA ANTIGUA	ANCIENT HISTORY
ATENAS	ATHENS
ENCANTADOR	CHARMING
COMPLEJO	COMPLEX
TASA DE MORTALIDAD	DEATH RATE
DECLIVE	DECLINE
VALLA, CERCA	FENCE
¡ ADELANTE !	GO AHEAD !
GRAFICO	GRAPH
CULPABLE	GUILTY
INSPECCION	INSPECTION
MONSTRUO	MONSTER
QUIOSCO	NEWSSTAND
RAZONABLEMENTE	REASONABLY
SEMINARIO	SEMINAR
ESTANTERIA	SHELF
A CORTO PLAZO	SHORT-RANGE
SEGURIDAD SOCIAL	SOCIAL SECURITY
MANCHA, PUNTO	SPOT
TECNICA	TECHNIQUE
LA MARINA	THE NAVY
LA VERDAD	THE TRUTH
NEUMATICOS	TIRES
CERA	WAX

	AMBIGUO	AMBIGUOUS
	VELA (DE CERA)	CANDLE
	TAPA, CUBIERTA	COVER
	CLIENTE	CUSTOMER
	ENTUSIASTA	ENTHUSIASTIC
	FIEBRE	FEVER
	PASILLO	HALLWAY
	TITULARES	HEADLINES
	IGNORANTE	IGNORANT
	JUEZ	JUDGE
	CUERO	LEATHER
	DESORDENADO	MESSY
	TIBURON	SHARK
	DISPARO	SHOT
	GAMBAS	SHRIMP
	ALGO ASI COMO ...	SOMETHING LIKE ...
	ESPIA	SPY
	TECNOLOGIA	TECHNOLOGY
	MOTIVAR	TO MOTIVATE
	AGRADAR, COMPLACER	TO PLEASE
	SEPARAR	TO SEPARATE
	ENVIAR (MERCANCIAS)	TO SHIP
	PROBLEMAS	TROUBLE
	MELODIA	TUNE
	RIQUEZA, PATRIMONIO	WEALTH

RETO, DESAFIO	CHALLENGE
CAMPEON	CHAMPION
CRISIS	CRISIS
MULTITUD	CROWD
EXIGENTE	DEMANDING
BASTANTE	FAIRLY
MODA	FASHION
PELEA, LUCHA	FIGHT
COMBUSTIBLE	FUEL
GRADUALMENTE	GRADUALLY
HECHO A MANO	HAND-MADE
IMPORTADOR	IMPORTER
INCENTIVO	INCENTIVE
LOGICO	LOGICAL
MOTIVADO	MOTIVATED
PERSONALMENTE	PERSONALLY
LA SOCIEDAD	SOCIETY
ESTABILIDAD	STABILITY
JOVEN DE 13 A 19 AÑOS	TEENAGER
RECONOCER, ADMITIR	TO ADMIT
HACER TURISMO	TO GO SIGHTSEEING
NOMBRAR	TO NAME
REFLEXIONAR	TO REFLECT
TUNEL	TUNNEL
ADINERADO	WEALTHY

	Spanish	English
	DESPISTADO	ABSENT-MINDED
	TELON DE FONDO, HISTORIAL	BACKGROUND
	BARBA	BEARD
	DE MEMORIA	BY HEART
	FECHADO	DATED
	DEFICIENTE	DEFICIENT
	ADJUNTO (EN UNA CARTA)	ENCLOSED
	AGRICULTOR	FARMER
	FINANCIERO	FINANCIAL
	ESPERANZA	HOPE
	CARCEL	JAIL
	MERMELADA	JAM
	MERCANCIAS	MERCHANDISE
	ASESINATO	MURDER
	PACIENCIA	PATIENCE
	PREVALENTE	PREVALENT
	PRIVILEGIADO	PRIVILEGED
	SEÑAL	SIGNAL
	TEMPERAMENTO	TEMPER
	ACONSEJAR	TO ADVISE
	RESULTAR UTIL	TO COME IN HANDY
	SELLAR	TO STAMP
	GEMELOS	TWINS
	ARMA	WEAPON
	¿ QUE CLASE DE ... ?	WHAT SORT OF ... ?

	LOGRO, CONSECUCION	ACHIEVEMENT
	PREMIO	AWARD
	COMPACTO	COMPACT
	CONFUNDIDO, CONFUSO	CONFUSED
	PRIMO	COUSIN
	DAÑO	DAMAGE
	DELICIOSO	DELICIOUS
	DESVENTAJA	DISADVANTAGE
	FURIOSO	FURIOUS
	GUAPO, DE BUEN VER	GOOD-LOOKING
	ILEGAL	ILLEGAL
	MENSUAL, MENSUALMENTE	MONTHLY
	CONCHA	SHELL
	SEDA	SILK
	VAPOR	STEAM
	TENDENCIA (PERSONAL)	TENDENCY
	ESO ES, EN EFECTO	THAT'S RIGHT
	EL HOMBRE DEL TIEMPO	THE WEATHERMAN
	SOÑAR	TO DREAM
	APAÑARSE, SALIR DEL PASO	TO GET BY
	COLGAR (EL TELEFONO)	TO HANG UP
	ASESINAR	TO MURDER
	REACCIONAR	TO REACT
	ESTABLECER, FIJAR	TO SET UP
	SUDAR	TO SWEAT

	GRACIOSO	AMUSING
	ARREGLO	ARRANGEMENT
	ENSEGUIDA	AT ONCE
	EN ESTOS MOMENTOS	AT PRESENT
	CATEDRAL	CATHEDRAL
	CEMENTO	CEMENT
	DIAMANTE	DIAMOND
	EFICACIA	EFFECTIVENESS
	ENTIDAD O PERSONA EMPLEADORA	EMPLOYER
	GRADUAL	GRADUAL
	PUERTO (DE MAR)	HARBOR
	PUNTO DE ENCUENTRO	MEETING PLACE
	MINISTERIO	MINISTRY
	MUSICO	MUSICIAN
	PREVENCION	PREVENTION
	CIENTIFICO	SCIENTIST
	SOMBRA	SHADOW
	SIMULTANEO	SIMULTANEOUS
	ACERO	STEEL
	FABULOSO	TERRIFIC
	EL DIABLO	THE DEVIL
	ABANDONAR, DARSE POR VENCIDO	TO GIVE UP
	RESOLVER, LIQUIDAR	TO SETTLE
	INCREIBLE	UNBELIEVABLE
	BODA	WEDDING

LIST 36

DE REPENTE	ALL OF A SUDDEN
AGRADECIMIENTO	APPRECIATION
SIGLO	CENTURY
DESORGANIZADO	DISORGANIZED
EXTREMADAMENTE	EXTREMELY
INSTALACIONES	FACILITIES
LA PESCA	FISHING
LLAMA	FLAME
AFORTUNADO	FORTUNATE
HUEVO DURO	HARD-BOILED EGG
INDIVIDUO	INDIVIDUAL
MONO	MONKEY
MISTERIO	MYSTERY
FISICO	PHYSICAL
SEVERO	SEVERE
SINCERO	SINCERE
EL LEJANO ORIENTE	THE FAR EAST
PROGRAMA, HORARIO	TIMETABLE
ESTAR EN CONTACTO CON	TO BE IN TOUCH WITH
TENER PUESTO (ROPA)	TO HAVE ON
HACER COMPRAS	TO SHOP
ALMACENAR	TO STORE
ENSAYAR, PONER A PRUEBA	TO TEST
INCOMODO	UNCOMFORTABLE
SEMANAL, SEMANALMENTE	WEEKLY

Vocabulary booklet 4

NIVEL AVANZADO

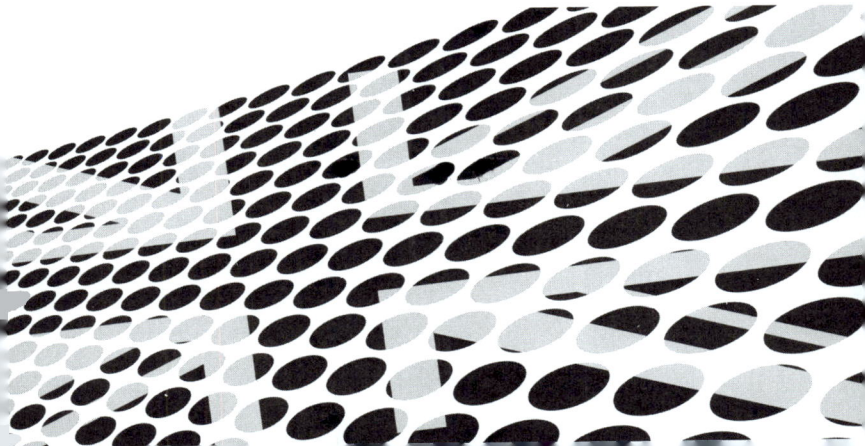

LIST I

1.	UN GRAN AVANCE CIENTIFICO	A BREAKTHROUGH
2.	ANSIOSO	ANXIOUS
3.	BIOLOGIA	BIOLOGY
4.	QUEJA	COMPLAINT
5.	CURRICULUM VITAE	CV
6.	ENANO	DWARF
7.	EL DESTINO	FATE
8.	COSECHA, RECOLECCION	HARVEST
9.	A CAMARA LENTA	IN SLOW MOTION
10.	DOTES DE MANDO	LEADERSHIP
11.	LA NATURALEZA	NATURE
12.	GRUPO DE PRESION	PRESSURE GROUP
13.	LA JUBILACION	RETIREMENT
14.	DOMINIO DE SI MISMO	SELF-RESTRAINT
15.	RESBALADIZO	SLIPPERY
16.	FUERZA	STRENGTH
17.	EL PADRE NUESTRO	THE LORD'S PRAYER
18.	NOMBRAR	TO APPOINT
19.	RESULTAR UTIL	TO COME IN HANDY
20.	APAÑARSE, SALIR DEL PASO	TO GET BY
21.	REMATAR	TO NAIL DOWN
22.	TROPEZAR CON, ENCONTRARSE CON	TO RUN INTO
23.	TARTAMUDEAR	TO STUTTER
24.	SOMETERSE A	TO UNDERGO
25.	INOLVIDABLE	UNFORGETTABLE

UN INCONVENIENTE	A DRAWBACK
DISCULPA	APOLOGY
CHANTAJE	BLACKMAIL
CUMPLIMIENTO	COMPLIANCE
CINICO	CYNICAL
JUBILACION ANTICIPADA	EARLY RETIREMENT
PLUMA	FEATHER
MAITRE	HEAD WAITER
MIENTRAS TANTO	IN THE MEANTIME
OCIO	LEISURE
DESATENCION, ABANDONO	NEGLECT
PROCEDIMIENTO	PROCEDURE
INGRESOS	REVENUE
AUTO-SUFICIENTE	SELF-SUFFICIENT
CHAPUCERO	SLOPPY
CARGADO (EL AMBIENTE)	STUFFY
LA LETRA (DE UNA CANCION)	THE LYRICS
VALORAR, TASAR	TO APPRAISE
SUICIDARSE	TO COMMIT SUICIDE
LIARSE, CONFUNDIRSE	TO GET MIXED UP
DESATENDER, NO CUMPLIR	TO NEGLECT
DIRIGIR EL COTARRO	TO RUN THE SHOW
SUBVENCIONAR	TO SUBSIDIZE
MINAR	TO UNDERMINE
IMPROBABLE	UNLIKELY

LIST 3

1.	UN BOCAZAS	A LOUDMOUTH
2.	POR LO VISTO, AL PARECER	APPARENTLY
3.	MEZCLA	BLEND
4.	CUMPLIDO	COMPLIMENT
5.	DANES	DANISH
6.	TERREMOTO	EARTHQUAKE
7.	CARACTERISTICAS	FEATURES
8.	ENCABEZAMIENTO	HEADING
9.	EN MEDIO	IN THE WAY
10.	PERMISIVO	LENIENT
11.	NO OBSTANTE	NEVERTHELESS
12.	PERFIL	PROFILE
13.	MARCHA ATRAS	REVERSE
14.	EGOISTA	SELFISH
15.	RANURA	SLOT
16.	SUBVENCION	SUBSIDY
17.	LA VIA LACTEA	THE MILKY WAY
18.	AGRADECER	TO APPRECIATE
19.	CUMPLIR CON	TO COMPLY WITH
20.	DESHACERSE DE	TO GET RID OF
21.	ORIENTAR	TO ORIENT
22.	OXIDARSE	TO RUST
23.	TENER EXITO, TRIUNFAR	TO SUCCEED
24.	SUBVALORAR	TO UNDERRATE
25.	VENIDERO	UPCOMING

UN ALIVIO	A RELIEF
APERITIVO	APPETIZER
BENDICION	BLESSING
CONSUMO	CONSUMPTION
PROCESO DE DATOS	DATA PROCESSING
TRANQUILO	EASY-GOING
HONORARIOS	FEE
LUCES (DEL COCHE)	HEADLIGHTS
PARIENTES POLITICOS	IN-LAWS
PALANCA	LEVER
QUIOSCO DE PRENSA	NEWSSTAND
BENEFICIO Y PERDIDA	PROFIT AND LOSS
GRATIFICANTE	REWARDING
PUNTO Y COMA	SEMICOLON
MAQUINA TRAGAPERRAS	SLOT MACHINE
DE EXITO, EXITOSO	SUCCESSFUL
LA MORALEJA	THE MORAL
DISCUTIR (ACALORADAMENTE)	TO ARGUE
DAR LA ENHORABUENA	TO CONGRATULATE
DESVESTIRSE	TO GET UNDRESSED
SOBREVIVIR A (UNA PERSONA)	TO OUTLIVE
BUSCAR	TO SEEK
DEMANDAR, PEDIR PLEITO	TO SUE
EMPRENDER	TO UNDERTAKE
LA CLASE ALTA	UPPER CLASS

LIST 5

1.	UN RECORDATORIO	A REMINDER
2.	CANDIDATO, SOLICITANTE	APPLICANT
3.	TENSION SANGUINEA	BLOOD PRESSURE
4.	PREOCUPADO	CONCERNED
5.	GUARDERIA	DAYCARE CENTER
6.	ECONOMICAS	ECONOMICS
7.	PROMETIDO / A	FIANCÉ
8.	ARDOR (DE ESTOMAGO)	HEART BURN
9.	INPRECISO	INACCURATE
10.	ESPERANZA DE VIDA	LIFE EXPECTANCY
11.	VIDA NOCTURNA	NIGHT LIFE
12.	RENTABILIDAD	PROFITABILITY
13.	ACERTIJO	RIDDLE
14.	ANTIGÜEDAD (EN UNA EMPRESA)	SENIORITY
15.	CARACOL	SNAIL
16.	BRONCEADO	SUNTAN
17.	LOS JUEGOS OLIMPICOS	THE OLYMPIC GAMES
18.	EVALUAR, VALORAR	TO ASSESS
19.	TOSER	TO COUGH
20.	REGALAR (POR NO QUERER)	TO GIVE AWAY
21.	SUPERAR	TO OVERCOME
22.	DAR EJEMPLO	TO SET AN EXAMPLE
23.	RESUMIR	TO SUM UP
24.	DESATAR	TO UNTIE
25.	ASPIRADORA	VACUUM CLEANER

UN TIMO	A RIP-OFF
VALORACION	APPRAISAL
GUARDA ESPALDAS	BODYGUARD
HORMIGON	CONCRETE
CALLEJON SIN SALIDA	DEAD END
BORDE	EDGE
SOLOMILLO	FILET MIGNON
AJETREADO	HECTIC
IMPUESTO SOBRE LA RENTA	INCOME TAX
PROBABILIDAD	LIKELIHOOD
TONTERIAS	NONSENSE
RENTABLE	PROFITABLE
ENSEGUIDA	RIGHT AWAY
HASTA LA VISTA	SO LONG
SOBERBIO (EXCELENTE)	SUPERB
LA PESTE	THE PLAGUE
ADJUDICAR, PREMIAR	TO AWARD
CONTAR CON	TO COUNT ON
CEDER, RENDIRSE	TO GIVE IN
SOBRESTIMAR	TO OVERESTIMATE
ASENTAR LA CABEZA	TO SETTLE DOWN
MANTENER, APOYAR	TO SUPPORT
DESENVOLVER	TO UNWRAP
VALIOSO	VALUABLE
SENSIBLE	SENSITIVE

LIST 7

	Spanish	English
1	UN CONTRATIEMPO	A SETBACK
2	AGRADECIDO	APPRECIATIVE
3	MOLESTO	BOTHERSOME
4	CONCIENZUDO	CONSCIENTIOUS
5	FECHA TOPE, PLAZO	DEADLINE
6	EFICAZ	EFFECTIVE
7	FLOTA	FLEET
8	HEREDERO	HEIR
9	CADA VEZ MAS	INCREASINGLY
10	PROBABLE	LIKELY
11	BLOC PARA NOTAS	NOTEPAD
12	PROMETEDOR	PROMISING
13	RIVALIDAD	RIVALRY
14	ACUERDO, ARREGLO	SETTLEMENT
15	BLANDURA	SOFTNESS
16	EXCEDENTE	SURPLUS
17	LA CRUZ ROJA	THE RED CROSS
18	APOYAR, RESPALDAR	TO BACK UP
19	CHOCAR	TO CRASH
20	HACER EL GANSO	TO GOOF OFF
21	DESBORDAR	TO OVERFLOW
22	AFILAR, SACAR PUNTA	TO SHARPEN
23	RENDIRSE	TO SURRENDER
24	PERDER TIEMPO (MALGASTAR)	TO WASTE TIME
25	VIABILIDAD	VIABILITY

	UN INCORDION	A TROUBLE MAKER
	ENFOQUE, PLANTEAMIENTO	APPROACH
	BRISA	BREEZE
	CONSULTOR	CONSULTANT
	MORTAL	DEADLY
	EFICAZMENTE	EFFECTIVELY
	CARNE Y HUESO	FLESH AND BLOOD
	SERVICIAL	HELPFUL
	INFLUYENTE	INFLUENTIAL
	PRESTAMO	LOAN
	HOGAR DE ANCIANOS	NURSING HOME
	PERSPECTIVAS	PROSPECTS
	RUTA	ROUTE
	COLONIZADOR	SETTLER
	SUELO (AGRICOLA)	SOIL
	ALREDEDORES	SURROUNDINGS
	LOS RESTOS	THE REMAINS
	REGATEAR	TO BARGAIN
	TACHAR	TO CROSS OUT
	AGARRAR	TO GRAB
	SOLAPARSE	TO OVERLAP
	DAR CARRETE	TO SHOOT THE BULL
	RODEAR	TO SURROUND
	DEBILITAR	TO WEAKEN
	VIABLE	VIABLE

LIST 9

1.	ACENTO	ACCENT
2.	APROPIADAMENTE	APPROPRIATELY
3.	DE MENTE AMPLIA	BROAD-MINDED
4.	CONSUMIDOR	CONSUMER
5.	SORDO	DEAF
6.	EFICACIA	EFFECTIVENESS
7.	INUNDACION	FLOOD
8.	DESAMPARADO	HELPLESS
9.	INGENIO	INGENUITY
10.	LANGOSTA (DE MAR)	LOBSTER
11.	PULPO	OCTOPUS
12.	ORGULLOSO	PROUD
13.	REALEZA	ROYALTY
14.	INDEMNIZACION POR DESPIDO	SEVERANCE PAY
15.	AGRIO	SOUR
16.	ENCUESTA, SONDEO	SURVEY
17.	CUANTO ANTES MEJOR	THE SOONER THE BETTER
18.	ESTAR EN MEDIO	TO BE IN THE WAY
19.	RECORTAR, REDUCIR	TO CUT BACK
20.	QUEJARSE	TO GRIPE
21.	DERROCAR	TO OVERTHROW
22.	ACORTAR	TO SHORTEN
23.	BARRER	TO SWEEP
24.	ENSANCHAR	TO WIDEN
25.	CIRCULO VICIOSO	VICIOUS CIRCLE

1	ALOJAMIENTO	ACCOMMODATIONS
2	ARABE (EL IDIOMA)	ARABIC
3	ESCOBA	BROOM
4	CONCURSO	CONTEST
5	SORDOMUDO	DEAF-MUTE
6	VIOLENTO, EMBARAZOSO	EMBARRASSING
7	INUNDADO	FLOODED
8	HERENCIA CULTURAL	HERITAGE
9	HERENCIA (DINERARIA)	INHERITANCE
10	CERRADURA	LOCK
11	LA VEJEZ	OLD AGE
12	SIEMPRE QUE	PROVIDED THAT
13	BASURA	RUBBISH
14	VERGÜENZA	SHAME
15	RUEDA DE REPUESTO	SPARE TIRE
16	PANTANO, CIENAGA	SWAMP
17	EL TERCER MUNDO	THE THIRD WORLD
18	ESTAR HECHO UN LIO	TO BE MIXED UP
19	TRATAR CON	TO DEAL WITH
20	DAÑAR	TO HARM
21	ABRUMAR	TO OVERWHELM
22	PRESUMIR, FARDAR	TO SHOW OFF
23	ACOMETER, RESOLVER	TO TACKLE
24	SER TESTIGO DE	TO WITNESS
25	VINO AÑEJO	VINTAGE WINE

LIST 11

	EN CONSECUENCIA	ACCORDINGLY
	GAMA, SURTIDO	ARRAY
	BUROCRACIA	BUREAUCRACY
	CHIRIMBOLO	CONTRAPTION
	ENCANTADO	DELIGHTED
	ANIMO, ALIENTO	ENCOURAGEMENT
	GOMA ESPUMA	FOAM RUBBER
	DUDOSO	HESITANT
	LESIONADO	INJURED
	LOGISTICA	LOGISTICS
	EN CAMBIO	ON THE OTHER HAND
	MARIONETA	PUPPET
	RUINAS	RUINS
	VERGONZOSO	SHAMEFUL
	CHISPA	SPARK
	CISNE	SWAN
	EL ESTADO DEL BIENESTAR	THE WELFARE STATE
	SER GORDO	TO BE OVERWEIGHT
	CONSIDERAR	TO DEEM
	PASARSELO BIEN	TO HAVE A GOOD TIME
	FALLECER	TO PASS AWAY
	SUSPIRAR	TO SIGH
	ECHAR LA SIESTA	TO TAKE A NAP
	RESOLVER	TO WORK OUT
	VOLCAN	VOLCANO

LIST 12

	Spanish	English
	RESPONSABLE	ACCOUNTABLE
	ARTIFICIAL	ARTIFICIAL
	ENTIERRO	BURIAL
	CONTROVERSIA	CONTROVERSY
	ENCANTADOR	DELIGHTFUL
	ALENTADOR	ENCOURAGING
	PARA SIEMPRE	FOR GOOD
	PUEBLO NATAL	HOME TOWN
	LOCO	INSANE
	A LARGO LAZO	LONG-RANGE
	OPTIMISMO	OPTIMISM
	MONEDERO	PURSE
	REGLA (PARA MEDIR)	RULER
	COBIJO	SHELTER
	ESPECIAS	SPICES
	SUDOR	SWEAT
	POR LO TANTO	THEREFORE
	ESTAR BAJO JURAMENTO	TO BE UNDER OATH
	ENCANTAR	TO DELIGHT
	INCAPACITAR	TO INCAPACITATE
	PELAR	TO PEEL
	APUNTARSE PARA	TO SIGN UP FOR
	APROVECHARSE DE	TO TAKE ADVANTAGE OF
	CONCLUIR	TO WRAP UP
	VOLUNTARIO	VOLUNTEER

1	PRECISION	ACCURACY
2	QUE YO SEPA	AS FAR AS I KNOW
3	CATOLICO	CATHOLIC
4	COMODIDAD	CONVENIENCE
5	EXIGENTE	DEMANDING
6	FONDO, AGUANTE	ENDURANCE
7	POR AHORA, DE MOMENTO	FOR THE TIME BEING
8	GANCHO, ANZUELO, GARFIO	HOOK
9	LOCURA	INSANITY
10	A LARGO PLAZO	LONG-TERM
11	DE OTRO MODO, SI NO	OTHERWISE
12	BASTANTES	QUITE A FEW
13	RON	RUM
14	JEREZ	SHERRY
15	PICANTE, CONDIMENTADO	SPICY
16	SUDOROSO	SWEATY
17	TOZUDO	THICK-HEADED
18	DERROTAR	TO BEAT
19	EXIGIR	TO DEMAND
20	INSINUAR	TO INSINUATE
21	IRSE AMONTONANDO	TO PILE UP
22	INCORPORARSE	TO SIT UP
23	PARECERSE A (FORMA DE SER)	TO TAKE AFTER
24	GRITAR	TO YELL
25	BUITRE	VULTURE

LOGRO	ACHIEVEMENT
APARTE DE	ASIDE FROM
GANADO VACUNO	CATTLE
COMODO, OPORTUNO	CONVENIENT
DESMORALIZANTE	DEMORALIZING
PROMETIDO (PARA CASARSE)	ENGAGED
CAPATAZ	FOREMAN
CLAXON, BOCINA	HORN
INVERSION	INVESTMENT
CHAPUCERO	LOUSY
SUPER POBLADO	OVERPOPULATED
MATERIAS PRIMAS	RAW MATERIALS
PISTA DE ATERRIZAJE	RUNWAY
ESCUDO	SHIELD
COLUMNA VERTEBRAL	SPINE
ESPADA	SWORD
ESPESURA, GROSOR	THICKNESS
MENDIGAR	TO BEG
PARTIR, SALIR	TO DEPART
GUARDAR UN SECRETO	TO KEEP A SECRET
RECALCAR, SEÑALAR	TO POINT OUT
ABOFETEAR	TO SLAP
DAR POR SENTADO	TO TAKE FOR GRANTED
TRABALENGUAS	TONGUE TWISTER
ADVERTENCIA	WARNING

1	TALON DE AQUILES	ACHILLES HEEL
2	ASFALTO	ASPHALT
3	ALTO EL FUEGO	CEASE-FIRE
4	CONVINCENTE	CONVINCING
5	DINAMARCA	DENMARK
6	NOVIAZGO FORMAL	ENGAGEMENT
7	VISION DE FUTURO, PREVISION	FORESIGHT
8	REHEN	HOSTAGE
9	IMPLICACION, INVOLUCRACION	INVOLVEMENT
10	LEAL	LOYAL
11	ABRUMADOR	OVERWHELMING
12	TRANQUILIZADOR	REASSURING
13	TRISTEZA	SADNESS
14	ESCASEZ (TEMPORAL)	SHORTAGE
15	PORTAVOZ	SPOKESMAN
16	PEZ ESPADA	SWORDFISH
17	COMPLETO Y ESMERADO	THOROUGH
18	DOBLAR	TO BEND
19	DESPLEGAR	TO DEPLOY
20	MANTENERSE EN FORMA	TO KEEP FIT
21	REZAR	TO PRAY
22	RESBALAR	TO SLIP
23	ASUMIR EL MANDO	TO TAKE OVER
24	DOLOR DE MUELA	TOOTHACHE
25	GARANTIA (SOBRE UN PRODUCTO)	WARRANTY

	Spanish	English
1	ACUSTICA	ACOUSTICS
2	VALORACION	ASSESSMENT
3	CELULA	CELL
4	GALLETA	COOKIE
5	PROFUNDIDAD	DEPTH
6	AGRADABLE	ENJOYABLE
7	PUNTO FUERTE	FORTE
8	VIVIENDA	HOUSING
9	CUESTION A DEBATIR	ISSUE
10	PULMONES	LUNGS
11	BUHO	OWL
12	TEMERARIO, MUY IMPRUDENTE	RECKLESS
13	BARCO DE VELA	SAILBOAT
14	ESCOPETA	SHOTGUN
15	PATROCINADOR	SPONSOR
16	CAMISETA	T-SHIRT
17	PURA SANGRE	THOROUGHBRED
18	TRAICIONAR	TO BETRAY
19	MERECER	TO DESERVE
20	MANTENERSE CON (EL RITMO)	TO KEEP UP WITH
21	PREDICAR	TO PREACH
22	SOSPECHAR ALGO	TO SMELL A RAT
23	TOMAR MEDIDAS	TO TAKE STEPS
24	CEPILLO DE DIENTES	TOOTHBRUSH
25	AVISPA	WASP

1	ADQUISICION	ACQUISITION
2	A TODA COSTA	AT ALL COSTS
3	RETO, DESAFIO	CHALLENGE
4	POLICIA	COP
5	MERECEDOR	DESERVING
6	EMPRENDEDOR	ENTERPRISING
7	QUINCENA	FORTNIGHT
8	¿ POR QUE ?	HOW COME ?
9	NO TIENE SENTIDO	IT DOESN'T MAKE ANY SENSE
10	LUJOSO	LUXURIOUS
11	OSTRA	OYSTER
12	RECREO	RECREATION
13	AHORROS	SAVINGS
14	PALA	SHOVEL
15	CÓNYUGE	SPOUSE
16	MANTEL	TABLECLOTH
17	ESMERO	THOROUGHNESS
18	CHANTAJEAR	TO BLACKMAIL
19	ODIAR	TO DESPISE
20	ECHAR A PATADAS	TO KICK OUT
21	ANDAR CON DILACIONES, APLAZAR	TO PROCRASTINATE
22	RONCAR	TO SNORE
23	RASGAR, ROMPER (TELA, PAPEL)	TO TEAR
24	PASTA DE DIENTES	TOOTHPASTE
25	PAPELERA	WASTE BASKET

Vocabulary Booklet | 139

1	AVANCE	ADVANCEMENT
2	EN EL MEJOR DE LOS CASOS	AT BEST
3	TRAMPOSO	CHEATER
4	COBRE	COPPER
5	PERJUDICIAL	DETRIMENTAL
6	ENTUSIASMO	ENTHUSIASM
7	CIMIENTOS	FOUNDATION
8	ENORME	HUGE
9	ME SUENA	IT RINGS A BELL
10	LUJO	LUXURY
11	INDOLORO	PAINLESS
12	ARBITRO	REFEREE
13	SIERRA (HERRAMIENTA)	SAW
14	ASTUTO	SHREWD
15	MONTON	STACK
16	HECHO A MEDIDA	TAILOR-MADE
17	CONSIDERADO	THOUGHTFUL
18	SANGRAR	TO BLEED
19	CAVAR	TO DIG
20	SECUESTRAR	TO KIDNAP
21	BENEFICIARSE DE	TO PROFIT FROM
22	ABLANDAR	TO SOFTEN
23	TOMAR EL PELO	TO TEASE
24	PALILLO	TOOTHPICK
25	DEBILIDAD	WEAKNESS

1	VENTAJOSO	ADVANTAGEOUS
2	DETENIDAMENTE	AT LENGTH
3	TALONARIO DE CHEQUES	CHECKBOOK
4	CORCHO	CORK
5	DISPOSITIVO	DEVICE
6	ENTORNO, MEDIO AMBIENTE	ENVIRONMENT
7	ASUSTADO	FRIGHTENED
8	HUMILDE	HUMBLE
9	¡ MENOS MAL !	IT'S A GOOD THING !
10	VALOR DE MERCADO	MARKET VALUE
11	LORO	PARROT
12	REFERENCIA	REFERRAL
13	CABEZA DE TURCO	SCAPEGOAT
14	TIMIDO	SHY
15	ESTANCADO	STAGNANT
16	MANSO	TAME
17	CONSIDERACION	THOUGHTFULNESS
18	FAROLEAR	TO BLUFF
19	ELABORAR, CONFECCIONAR	TO DRAW UP
20	DESPEDIR (EN MASA)	TO LAY OFF
21	PROPORCIONAR	TO PROVIDE
22	RESOLVER	TO SOLVE
23	PENSAR EN VOZ ALTA	TO THINK OUT LOUD
24	TORNEO	TOURNAMENT
25	ADINERADO, RICO	WEALTHY

1	ADVERSO	ADVERSE
2	AL AZAR	AT RANDOM
3	CUENTA CORRIENTE	CHECKING ACCOUNT
4	SOCIEDAD ANONIMA	CORPORATION
5	INCAPACITADO	DISABLED
6	A LA LARGA	EVENTUALLY
7	BENEFICIOS SOCIALES DE NOMINA	FRINGE BENEFITS
8	SUPONGO QUE SI	I GUESS SO
9	¡ YA ERA HORA !	IT'S ABOUT TIME !
10	DOMINIO	MASTERY
11	CONTRASEÑA	PASSWORD
12	INDEPENDIENTEMENTE DE	REGARDLESS OF
13	CICATRIZ	SCAR
14	REPUGNANTE, NAUSEABUNDO	SICKENING
15	MANCHA	STAIN
16	MANDARINA	TANGERINE
17	HILO	THREAD
18	SONROJARSE	TO BLUSH
19	GOTEAR	TO DRIP
20	OMITIR	TO LEAVE OUT
21	RECURRIR A ENCHUFES	TO PULL STRINGS
22	RESOLVER	TO SORT OUT
23	REFLEXIONAR SOBRE	TO THINK OVER
24	GRUA (PARA REMOLCAR)	TOW TRUCK
25	¡ VAYA FOLLON !	WHAT A MESS !

LIST 21

■	CONSEJO, ASESORAMIENTO	ADVICE
■	A EXPENSAS DE	AT THE EXPENSE OF
■	LISTA DE VERIFICACION	CHECKLIST
■	COSTOSO	COSTLY
■	DECEPCIONADO	DISAPPOINTED
■	DE VEZ EN CUANDO	EVERY NOW AND THEN
■	BRECHA, LAGUNA	GAP
■	TENGO UN HAMBRE QUE NO VEAS	I'M STARVING
■	NO VALE LA PENA	IT'S NOT WORTH IT
■	COLCHON	MATTRESS
■	NOMINA	PAYROLL
■	LAMENTABLE	REGRETFUL
■	ESPANTA PAJAROS	SCARECROW
■	PECADO	SIN
■	FONDO, AGUANTE	STAMINA
■	AGUA DE GRIFO	TAP WATER
■	AMENAZA	THREAT
■	HERVIR	TO BOIL
■	DARSE DE BAJA	TO DROP OUT
■	ALARGAR	TO LENGTHEN
■	DAR UN PUÑETAZO	TO PUNCH
■	DERRAMAR, TIRAR	TO SPILL
■	AMENAZAR	TO THREATEN
■	CHALET ADOSADO	TOWNHOUSE
■	CAPRICHOSO	WHIMSICAL

	Spanish	English
1	AFABLE	AFFABLE
2	ATLETA	ATHLETE
3	QUIMICA	CHEMISTRY
4	TUTOR	COUNSELOR
5	DECEPCION	DISAPPOINTMENT
6	DE VEZ EN CUANDO	EVERY ONCE IN A WHILE
7	DOTADO	GIFTED
8	ANALFABETO	ILLITERATE
9	CONCEPTO, PARTIDA	ITEM
10	LIO, FOLLON, DESORDEN	MESS
11	PEATON	PEDESTRIAN
12	PARIENTES, FAMILIARES	RELATIVES
13	BUFANDA	SCARF
14	PECADOR	SINNER
15	HOMBRE DE ESTADO	STATESMAN
16	FECHA OBJETIVO	TARGET DATE
17	AMENAZADOR	THREATENING
18	AUMENTAR	TO BOOST
19	AHOGARSE	TO DROWN
20	DECEPCIONAR	TO LET DOWN
21	APLAZAR	TO PUT OFF
22	ESCUPIR	TO SPIT
23	ORGANIZAR UNA FIESTA	TO THROW A PARTY
24	ATLETISMO	TRACK AND FIELD
25	LATIGO	WHIP

1	ACOMODADO	AFFLUENT
2	INTENTO	ATTEMPT
3	BARBILLA	CHIN
4	MOSTRADOR	COUNTER
5	DESANIMADO	DISCOURAGED
6	UN DIA SI Y OTRO NO	EVERY OTHER DAY
7	CHISMORREO	GOSSIP
8	DESEQUILIBRIO	IMBALANCE
9	MARFIL	IVORY
10	DESORDENADO	MESSY
11	SEMEJANTES	PEERS
12	FIABILIDAD	RELIABILITY
13	PLAN	SCHEME
14	UN ESCEPTICO	A SKEPTIC
15	CONSTANTE Y EQUILIBRADO	STEADY
16	SABROSO	TASTY
17	UMBRAL	THRESHOLD
18	BOTAR	TO BOUNCE
19	TEÑIR	TO DYE
20	TUMBARSE	TO LIE DOWN
21	REUNIR LAS CONDICIONES	TO QUALIFY
22	RIZAR EL RIZO	TO SPLIT HAIRS
23	TIRAR (A LA BASURA)	TO THROW AWAY
24	REMOLQUE	TRAILER
25	SILBATO, PITO	WHISTLE

	Spanish	English
	AGRESIVO	AGGRESSIVE
	ABOGADO	ATTORNEY
	NOCHE BUENA	CHRISTMAS EVE
	PAISAJE	COUNTRYSIDE
	DESALENTADOR	DISCOURAGING
	EXAGERACION	EXAGGERATION
	ESTUDIOS DE POSGRADO	GRADUATE STUDIES
	IMPRESIONANTE	IMPRESSIVE
	FRASCO	JAR
	RESERVAS, RECELOS	MISGIVINGS
	PESETERO	PENNY PINCHER
	FIABLE	RELIABLE
	BECA	SCHOLARSHIP
	ESCEPTICO	SKEPTICAL
	EMPINADO	STEEP
	DECLARACION DE LA RENTA	TAX RETURN
	AHORRATIVO	THRIFTY
	SOBORNAR	TO BRIBE
	ABRAZAR	TO EMBRACE
	COJEAR	TO LIMP
	DESHACERSE EN ELOGIOS SOBRE	TO RAVE ABOUT
	EXPRIMIR	TO SQUEEZE
	DEVOLVER, VOMITAR	TO THROW UP
	TRAIDOR	TRAITOR
	AL POR MAYOR	WHOLESALE

OBJETIVO	AIM
DOLOR DE ESPALDA	BACKACHE
ALMEJAS	CLAMS
VALOR, VALENTIA	COURAGE
DESCUBRIMIENTO	DISCOVERY
AGOTADO, RENDIDO	EXHAUSTED
PROMOCION (ESCOLAR)	GRADUATING CLASS
INAPROPIADO	IMPROPER
POR SI ACASO	JUST IN CASE
ENGAÑOSO	MISLEADING
BUENA SALUD FISICA	PHYSICAL FITNESS
DIGNO DE ELOGIO	REMARKABLE
TIJERAS	SCISSORS
ESCEPTICISMO	SKEPTICISM
VOLANTE	STEERING WHEEL
CONTRIBUYENTE	TAXPAYER
TRONO	THRONE
CRIAR, EDUCAR	TO BRING UP
PERMITIR, POSIBILITAR	TO ENABLE
ESPERAR CON ILUSION	TO LOOK FORWARD TO
REACCIONAR	TO REACT
APUÑALAR	TO STAB
HACER COSQUILLAS	TO TICKLE
PERIODO DE PRUEBA	TRIAL PERIOD
MAYORISTA	WHOLESALER

1	PASILLO (AVION, CINE, ETC.)	AISLE
2	TRABAJO RETRASADO ACUMULADO	BACKLOG
3	COMPAÑERO DE CLASE	CLASSMATE
4	COBARDE	COWARD
5	ENFERMEDAD	DISEASE
6	CUENTA DE GASTOS	EXPENSE ACCOUNT
7	GRATIFICANTE	GRATIFYING
8	EN UN APRIETO	IN A BIND
9	RODILLA	KNEE
10	MALENTENDIDO	MISUNDERSTANDING
11	FISICA	PHYSICS
12	CONTROL REMOTO	REMOTE CONTROL
13	PAPEL DE BORRADOR	SCRATCH PAPER
14	MAÑOSO	SKILLFUL
15	TALLO	STEM
16	TENTADOR	TEMPTING
17	DEDO PULGAR	THUMB
18	REVENTAR	TO BURST
19	EVOLUCIONAR, DESARROLLAR	TO EVOLVE
20	INVESTIGAR	TO LOOK INTO
21	DARSE CUENTA DE	TO REALIZE
22	MANCHAR	TO STAIN
23	ATAR CABOS SUELTOS	TO TIE LOOSE ENDS
24	TRIBU	TRIBE
25	PELUCA	WIG

1	ALIANZA	ALLIANCE
2	GLOBO	BALLOON
3	PRECIPICIO, ACANTILADO	CLIFF
4	CANGREJO, NECORA	CRAB
5	VERGONZOSO	DISGRACEFUL
6	EXPERIMENTADO	EXPERIENCED
7	TUMBA	GRAVE
8	EN UN APRIETO	IN A PINCH
9	NUDO	KNOT
10	MONOPOLIO	MONOPOLY
11	RATERO, CARTERISTA	PICKPOCKET
12	ELIMINACION	REMOVAL
13	DESTORNILLADOR	SCREWDRIVER
14	FLACO	SKINNY
15	ESTEREOTIPO	STEREOTYPE
16	TIERNO	TENDER
17	APRETADO	TIGHT
18	EXIGIR	TO CALL FOR
19	SOBRESALIR, DESTACAR	TO EXCEL
20	PARECERSE A	TO LOOK LIKE
21	NEGARSE A	TO REFUSE
22	DESTACAR, SOBRESALIR	TO STAND OUT
23	ANDAR DE PUNTILLAS	TO TIPTOE
24	TRAMPOSO	TRICKY
25	PRUDENTE, JUICIOSO, SABIO	WISE

ALIADO	ALLY
EN QUIEBRA	BANKRUPT
ARMARIO	CLOSET
GRIETA	CRACK
DISFRAZ	DISGUISE
PERICIA, HABILIDAD	EXPERTISE
GRASIENTO	GREASY
POR ADELANTADO	IN ADVANCE
CONOCIMIENTOS	KNOWHOW
ES MAS	MOREOVER
PALOMA	PIGEON
DE RENOMBRE	RENOWNED
GUION	SCRIPT
RASCACIELOS	SKYSCRAPER
ESTOFADO	STEW
PROVISIONAL	TENTATIVE
ESTAÑO	TIN
CANCELAR	TO CALL OFF
SALIR	TO EXIT
FORRARSE	TO MAKE A KILLING
ARREPENTIRSE	TO REGRET
PARTIR DE CERO	TO START FROM SCRATCH
LANZAR UNA MONEDA AL AIRE	TO TOSS A COIN
TROPAS	TROOPS
GUSANO, LOMBRIZ	WORM

ALMENDRA	ALMOND
CEBADA	BARLEY
PISTA, INDICIO	CLUE
CHOQUE	CRASH
INSATISFECHO	DISSATISFIED
FECHA DE CADUCIDAD	EXPIRATION DATE
AVARO	GREEDY
EN CUALQUIER CASO	IN ANY CASE
EXPERTO	KNOWLEDGEABLE
HIPOTECA	MORTGAGE
PELIGRO, ESCOLLO, TRAMPA	PITFALL
RESERVADO	RESERVED
GAVIOTA	SEA GULL
CALUMNIA	SLANDER
PALO	STICK
FABULOSO, GENIAL	TERRIFIC
HASTA CIERTO PUNTO	TO A CERTAIN EXTENT
CALMARSE	TO CALM DOWN
ESFUMARSE	TO FADE AWAY
BURLARSE DE	TO MAKE FUN OF
SOLTAR, LIBERAR	TO RELEASE
SEGUIR EN CONTACTO	TO STAY IN TOUCH
ENDURECER	TO TOUGHEN
DIGNO DE CONFIANZA	TRUSTWORTHY
SIN VALOR	WORTHLESS

1	ALUMINIO	ALUMINUM
2	BARRERA	BARRIER
3	ENTRENADOR	COACH
4	TRIPULACION	CREW
5	BORRADOR	DRAFT
6	CABLE ALARGADOR	EXTENSION CORD
7	TASA DE CRECIMIENTO	GROWTH RATE
8	EN CUALQUIER CASO	IN ANY EVENT
9	ETIQUETA	LABEL
10	MAYORMENTE	MOSTLY
11	DE SOBRA	PLENTY OF
12	EMBALSE	RESERVOIR
13	FOCA	SEAL
14	SESGADO, PARCIAL	SLANTED
15	PEGAJOSO	STICKY
16	TEXTURA	TEXTURE
17	LOGRAR, CONSEGUIR	TO ACCOMPLISH
18	LLEVAR A CABO	TO CARRY OUT
19	FRACASAR	TO FAIL
20	CAUSAR PROBLEMAS	TO MAKE TROUBLE
21	DEPENDER DE, CONFIAR EN	TO RELY ON
22	PEGAR (CON PEGAMENTO)	TO STICK
23	REMOLCAR	TO TOW
24	MATRICULA, TASAS ACADEMICAS	TUITION
25	HERIDA	WOUND

1	SIMPATICO	AMIABLE
2	ALBORNOZ	BATHROBE
3	CARBON	COAL
4	COSECHA, CULTIVO	CROP
5	UN INCONVENIENTE	A DRAWBACK
6	INSTALACIONES	FACILITIES
7	DIRECTRICES	GUIDELINES
8	RESPONSABLE DE	IN CHARGE OF
9	CHULETAS DE CORDERO	LAMB CHOPS
10	LENGUA MATERNA	MOTHER TONGUE
11	ENCHUFE	PLUG
12	DE CARACTER FUERTE	RESILIENT
13	SEMILLAS	SEEDS
14	NEGRERO	SLAVE DRIVER
15	ROÑOSO	STINGY
16	LOS ARABES	THE ARABS
17	LOGRAR	TO ACHIEVE
18	ALCANZAR (DESDE ATRAS)	TO CATCH UP
19	DESMAYAR	TO FAINT
20	HACER USO DE	TO MAKE USE OF
21	RESCATAR	TO RESCUE
22	APESTAR	TO STINK
23	ATRAPAR	TO TRAP
24	ATUN, BONITO	TUNA
25	HERIDO	WOUNDED

UN CONOCIDO	AN ACQUAINTANCE
CARNE DE VACUNO	BEEF
COLEGA	COLLEAGUE
CRUCIGRAMA	CROSSWORD PUZZLE
TAMBOR	DRUM
FRACASO	FAILURE
CONEJILLO DE INDIAS	GUINEA PIG
EN DECLIVE	IN DECLINE
PAISAJE	LANDSCAPE
LEMA	MOTTO
FONTANERIA	PLUMBING
DECIDIDO, RESUELTO	RESOLUTE
EGOCENTRICO	SELF-CENTERED
ESCLAVITUD	SLAVERY
LA BOLSA	THE STOCK EXCHANGE
EL CANAL DE LA MANCHA	THE ENGLISH CHANNEL
ADMITIR, RECONOCER	TO ACKNOWLEDGE
CESAR	TO CEASE
VENIRSE ABAJO (UN PLAN)	TO FALL THROUGH
TACHAR	TO MARK OUT
JUBILARSE	TO RETIRE
ENDEREZAR	TO STRAIGHTEN
CONFIAR EN, FIARSE DE	TO TRUST
PROFESOR PARTICULAR	TUTOR
ARRUGAS	WRINKLES

UNA MOLESTIA	AN INCONVENIENCE
DE ANTEMANO	BEFOREHAND
ANUNCIO (EN TELEVISION)	COMMERCIAL
CRUCERO	CRUISE
TINTORERIA	DRY CLEANERS
JUEGO LIMPIO	FAIR PLAY
RESACA (POR BEBER MUCHO)	HANGOVER
EN PROFUNDIDAD	IN DEPTH
CARRIL	LANE
ALPINISTA	MOUNTAIN CLIMBER
OSO POLAR	POLAR BEAR
INGENIOSO, QUE TIENE RECURSOS	RESOURCEFUL
CONFIANZA EN UNO MISMO	SELF-CONFIDENCE
SOMNIFERO	SLEEPING PILL
TABURETE	STOOL
LA META	THE FINISH LINE
DIRIGIR. LA PALABRA A	TO ADDRESS
PERSEGUIR	TO CHASE
TENER GANAS DE	TO FEEL LIKE
CASAR, HACER JUEGO	TO MATCH
BATIRSE EN RETIRADA	TO RETREAT
FORTALECER	TO STRENGTHEN
PROBARSE	TO TRY ON
INDUDABLEMENTE	UNDOUBTEDLY
APUNTALO	WRITE IT DOWN

	Spanish	English
1	UN NUMERO IMPAR	AN ODD NUMBER
2	PERTENENCIAS	BELONGINGS
3	COMPROMISO	COMMITMENT
4	ADUANA	CUSTOMS
5	ABURRIDO	DULL
6	FE	FAITH
7	DAÑINO, PERJUDICIAL	HARMFUL
8	EN VIGOR	IN FORCE
9	RISA	LAUGHTER
10	PUERTO DE MONTAÑA	MOUNTAIN PASS
11	POLITICA (DE ACTUACION)	POLICY
12	RECURSOS	RESOURCES
13	TIMIDO, COHIBIDO	SELF-CONSCIOUS
14	ESBELTO	SLENDER
15	CIGÜEÑA	STORK
16	EL ESPIRITU SANTO	THE HOLY SPIRIT
17	LEVANTAR (UNA SESION)	TO ADJOURN
18	MASTICAR	TO CHEW
19	AVERIGUAR, ENTERARSE	TO FIND OUT
20	DERRETIR, FUNDIR	TO MELT
21	MODIFICAR	TO REVISE
22	HACER HUELGA	TO STRIKE
23	RECHAZAR, BAJAR (VOLUMEN)	TO TURN DOWN
24	INTRANQUILO, PREOCUPADO	UNEASY
25	RADIOGRAFIA	X-RAY

MOLESTO	ANNOYING
APUESTA	BET
COMPARACION	COMPARISON
RECORTE (PRESUPUESTARIO)	CUTBACK
TONTO	DUMB
FIEL	FAITHFUL
INOFENSIVO	HARMLESS
EN PRIVADO	IN PRIVATE
PLEITO, DEMANDA	LAWSUIT
CORDILLERA, SIERRA	MOUNTAIN RANGE
LA POLITICA	POLITICS
CURRICULUM VITAE	RÉSUMÉ
AUTO-ESTIMA	SELF-ESTEEM
LONCHA, REBANADA	SLICE
TORMENTOSO	STORMY
LA EDAD DEL HIELO	THE ICE AGE
ACONSEJAR, ASESORAR	TO ADVISE
DECLARAR (CON PRETENSIONES)	TO CLAIM
REUNIR	TO GATHER
FUSIONAR (EMPRESAS)	TO MERGE
CODEARSE CON	TO RUB SHOULDERS WITH
ESFORZARSE	TO STRIVE
APARECER, SUBIR (VOLUMEN)	TO TURN UP
EL PARO	UNEMPLOYMENT
YATE	YACHT

ANSIEDAD	ANXIETY
BIOLOGO	BIOLOGIST
COMPETITIVIDAD	COMPETITIVENESS
RECORTES	CUTBACKS
DEBER	DUTY
FALSO	FAKE
ASPERO	HARSH
EN RESUMIDAS CUENTAS	IN SHORT
CAPA	LAYER
INGENUO	NAÏVE
RECORTE DE PRENSA	PRESS CLIPPING
AL POR MENOR	RETAIL
INDEPENDIENTE Y SEGURO DE SI	SELF-RELIANT
ALPARGATAS	SLIPPERS
PAJA	STRAW
LA GOTA QUE COLMO EL VASO	THE LAST STRAW
SOLICITAR	TO APPLY FOR
ACLARAR	TO CLEAR UP
SALIR ADELANTE	TO GET AHEAD
TRASPAPELAR, PERDER	TO MISPLACE
DESCARTAR	TO RULE OUT
TROPEZAR	TO STUMBLE
SUBESTIMAR	TO UNDERESTIMATE
INJUSTO	UNFAIR
YA LO SUPERARAS	YOU'LL GET OVER IT

NOTAS

NOTAS